Gayle Smerdon PhD is a coach, speaker, author and organisational development practitioner who specialises in learning and culture. Gayle applies her expertise in strategic organisational development, learning, change and workplace communication, to create simple, practical tools and programs. Gayle is an enthusiastic advocate for lifelong learning; this commitment and passion motivated her to write *iDevelop*. She lives in Melbourne and delivers learning programs around the country.

www.gaylesmerdon.com
www.linkedin.com/in/gayle-smerdon/

iDEVELOP

How to take charge of your professional
development by becoming a conscious learner

Gayle Smerdon PhD

BROADCAST

*In memory of my dad,
whose belief in the importance of getting a good education
may have started this whole darn thing.*

The author has made every effort to contact copyright holders for material used in this book. Any person or organisation that may have been overlooked should contact the author.

First published in 2019 by Gayle Smerdon
www.gaylesmerdon.com

Copyright © 2019 Gayle Smerdon

The moral rights of the author have been asserted.

 A catalogue record for this book is available from the National Library of Australia

ISBN: 978-0-6480078-6-9 (Paperback)
ISBN: 978-0-6480078-7-6 (Ebook)

All rights reserved. Except as permitted under the Australian Copyright Act 1968 (for example, fair dealing for the purposes of study, research, criticism or review) no part of this book may be reproduced, stored in a retrieval system, communicated or transmitted in any form or by any means without prior written permission from the author. All enquires should be made to the author at hello@gaylesmerdon.com

Produced by Broadcast Books, www.broadcastbooks.com.au
Cover and text design by Seymour Design, seymourdesign.net
Typeset by Seymour Design
Author photograph by Alise Black, Alise Black Photographic Studio

CONTENTS

Introduction 1

Chapter 1   **Why learning matters now** 13

Chapter 2   **Learning 101** 23

Chapter 3   **The dynamics of learning** 43

Chapter 4   **Reflection** 51

Chapter 5   **Action** 61

Chapter 6   **Support** 79

Chapter 7   **What about me?** 95

Chapter 8   **Finding information** 119

Chapter 9   **What does 'good' content look like?** 137

Conclusion   Putting it all together 149

Endnotes   159

Index   163

INTRODUCTION

I've been a learner all my life. I'm addicted to formal and informal education. Some of my friends are worried the desire to learn might be pathological in my case! But what my concerned friends don't realise, and neither do a lot of people, is that we are all lifelong learners. It just so happens that some of us recognise this skill in ourselves and use it, and others are learning deniers.

Let's start under the house I grew up in, where the tall wooden stumps elevating the back of our home on the sloping block made an excellent space for playing and working. 'Under the house', as it was called, included the laundry, my dad's workshop and a racetrack for our tricycles. In the workshop were a couple of large tool cabinets mounted above a workbench. This is where Dad kept his extensive collection of equipment, which he used for building and repairing pretty much anything. He'd painted the cabinets doors with green chalkboard paint, and from the time I found out schools existed, I would line up all my dolls in their little chairs and teach them a range of erudite lessons. Don't laugh – some of those dolls are in Mensa now!

However, I often found primary and secondary school far less inspiring than the classes I offered my dolls. Sadly, this is an all too common experience. Although I have the highest regard for the teaching profession, a great deal of my problem had to do with a specific teacher at a critical time. For a while there, education and I broke up. We went our separate ways. But after some low-level jobs and a lot of fun travelling, we met up again and I continued my higher education, all the way through to PhD level. I even did a Graduate Diploma in Psychology for afters. At one stage, I thought of becoming an academic, but I found my vocation in the more practical field of learning and organisational development.

While I am a lifelong learner and work in the field, I don't necessarily think of myself as especially smart or clever. Any number of life choices would bear that out, and some friends and relatives would likely attest to it. I am often haunted by the same lack of confidence and uncertainty that a lot of people experience. But I also know that there are many different types of 'smart' and 'clever' and these words aren't the only ways, or best ways, to measure people.

I do what I do today because I find helping people grow through nurturing their curiosity – both focused inward and outward – highly rewarding. But I am not convinced that much of what people know about learning, and how it's applied, is useful. And I believe this contributes to people being learning deniers.

There are many reasons why someone might become a learning denier. The world we live, love and work in is going through rapid change. It's clear there is a need for us to become more conscious about how we learn if we want a chance at keeping up. But just keeping up and keeping sane seems to be getting trickier each day, and it takes quite a bit of work to navigate this landscape we've created. There is much we need to know, do and be in order to keep ourselves afloat in this world, even more so if we want to be able to help shape our place in it.

The work we do and the workplaces we do it in – businesses of all shapes and sizes, and across all industries – are undergoing change at an unprecedented pace. Many futurists and those in the prediction industry will tell you about the kinds of jobs that will be required and the skills you will need to master in order to manage this challenging future. And be in no doubt – that future is pretty much here right now.

You probably know this already. However, something you might not be aware of is that nurturing a stronger understanding of how we learn in order to learn better might just be the *single greatest competitive advantage* we have in the workplace. And learning smarter and better could improve our society and possibly save the world as we know it – but let's not get ahead of ourselves. Before we go global, let's see how learning can help you.

》

Whoever you are and whatever place you find yourself in right now in your career, there's never been a better time to take charge of your professional development. This book is here to help you be the best 'future you' possible – whether that means preparing for your next role, reinvigorating your current role, or simply helping you find good information about things that matter to you.

It's a practical guide to help you discover how *you* learn, so you can acquire new skills more readily or broaden and deepen your existing talents. Irrespective of what expertise you may need in the future, by understanding how you learn you will be ready and able to develop any skill more effectively.

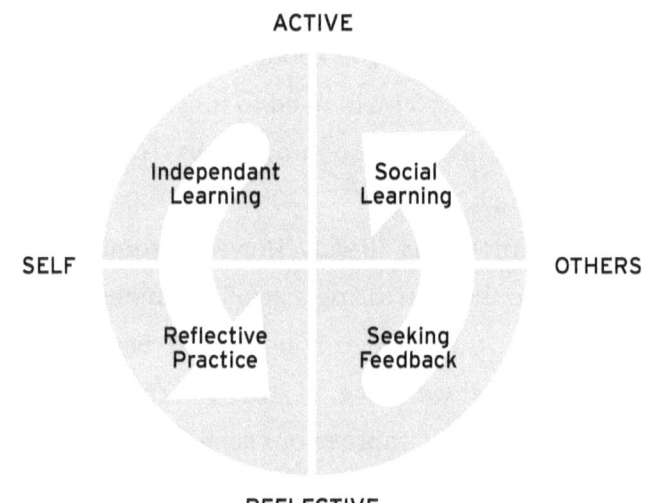

The *iDevelop* Learning Model

The approach we take here is based on three key ideas.
- The first is about *what* you are learning. People tend to learn best when they play a major role in deciding *what* they want to learn and are supported to learn it. We know this as 'self-directed' learning.

- The second looks at *who* is involved. This is about the need to balance independent learning (learning on one's own) and social learning (engaging with others).
- Finally, it also matters *how* you go about learning. You need to be able to actively engage in learning, reflect on what has been learnt and continue both in a virtuous cycle.

These key points may seem obvious to some. But one of the reasons learning deniers exist is because they might have had a poor experience in situations called 'learning'. And there can be many kinds of poor experience, especially in the workplace.

Learning deniers could be convinced they don't need to learn anything because they do the same thing every day. They might not want to learn anything because it is seen as something additional to the work they do – and there is already plenty of that. Perhaps the learning that is offered in their organisation doesn't readily translate to what they currently do, or is offered in only a few ways – online or in workshops, for example. Learning can sometimes feel 'unsafe' because the learner might need to admit they don't know something – and that is frightening for some people in some workplaces.

But what learning deniers often overlook is that learning is as natural as breathing. We do it whether we are conscious of it or not. We change whether we are conscious of changing or not. So, really, we don't just need new skills at work – we need to rethink the relationship between learning, work and change in our organisations. Learning happens in *and* outside of training rooms, conferences and the education sector. We naturally learn useful and harmful habits, behaviours and skills – but it's not always easy to know what works if we aren't aware of the nature of learning.

Becoming a conscious learner is, in my mind, the most important skill you can have. That's what this book is all about. That this makes us more attractive employees in the predicted future of work is only one benefit – and probably not the most important one. I believe that conscious learning has implications for organisations, employees, managers, CEOs and CFOs, as well as learning providers; but this book is not about them – it's about you.

iDevelop, whether read as the book you hold in your hands or experienced as a session with me in your workplace, is about learning how to learn, charting your own course and taking ownership of how you work. And it's about how you apply this knowledge to implement *Project You*.

Project You is concerned with building the skills and behaviours to help you be a better leader, teammate, colleague, employee, friend, family or community member. *Project You* is not a selfish endeavour; it's a chance for you to be your best. While focused on professional development, the positive changes *Project You* can help you make will directly or indirectly influence everything you do. And that's not a bad thing.

Throughout the book we will call your project '*Project You*' for convenience, but you should definitely give it a name, preferably something that makes you laugh or inspires you. (I'm looking for a new project right now with an acronym that spells PIG so I can tell myself I'm working on my little piggy!) It can be based on a long term goal – like 'Project Go Me' or 'Project CEO in 5'; or it could be based on whatever your ONE THING (which we will get to in a minute) is – like 'Project Love Public Speaking' or 'Project Guitar Hero'. And you can change it over time – because as you learn, you'll be changing too.

Now, iDevelop is designed to be a practical book, but, as the founder of social psychology Kurt Lewins says, 'There is nothing so practical as a good theory', so there is a bit of that as well. We investigate what underpins conscious learning and why it matters. We trek through a few useful ideas about how we learn – how our beliefs support our learning, for example – and we look at what makes learning sticky.

And then there's the fun part. Knowing about learning is great – especially if you are a people-nerd like me – but it will always mean more to us if we learn something for a reason. If it's a good reason, that's all the better. As you progress through the book, you are invited to apply what you learn to your big project – Project You. To begin Project You, you'll need to decide what to focus your learning on. This will be your ONE THING. It won't, however, be your only thing. You'll have many ONE THINGS over the course of Project You – it's an ongoing project, after all – but you start by choosing that first ONE THING to work on. Nifty.

So let's clarify things a little: this book is not about teaching you a specific skill, but about helping you find out how to develop any skill you want to learn. iDevelop is content agnostic – it doesn't know or care what that specific thing (your ONE THING) is or will be. It's here to help you find out how to learn that ONE THING, whatever it is.

You may already have an idea of what your ONE THING is, or

maybe it's hard for you to decide. For those who have difficulty finding their first ONE THING, *iDevelop* has some useful thoughts on that too. Determining what really matters to you, and how you want to be different as a result of your efforts, *Project You*, will help you to decide what your ONE THING will be.

Once you've picked the ONE THING you want to work on, the first thing you will need to do is ... nothing. We tend to want to rush into action, but for a successful *Project You*, you'll first need to spend some time observing what you already do. Your very first action is to build awareness. This is followed by research, choosing an action, and then testing it out. And, just like any other experiment, you'll reflect on the results, see what you need to adjust and then you'll be ready to take the next step.

It's also important that you don't do *Project You* totally alone. *iDevelop* shows you how to get advice and support from a few carefully chosen people in order to seek feedback and overcome any limits on your perspective on your ONE THING. This small, select group, which we will call *The Team*, will encourage you, share advice and hold you to account – because you can't do it all alone. Learning is a team game.

To understand how to make learning stick, *iDevelop* incorporates aspects of neuroscience, psychology and behavioural economics that can offer insights into what motivates us, keeps us focused and helps us build great learning habits. As making changes and learning new things requires effort, you'll want to make your new skill or behaviours as automatic as possible, so it becomes your new way of being. You'll want to recall what you need when you need to.

Understanding the practical applications of these new insights can help speed your progress and make it more lasting.

To help you keep track of your *Project You* journey, we've also put a handy step-by-step guide at the end of the book (The *Project You* Guide). While, hopefully, you will be putting what you learn into practice as you work through the chapters, the guide offers a concise overview and an easy reference for those who like to see useful information at a glance, or who prefer using a checklist. Plus, there is some gentle encouragement to help you think about what's next after you complete your first ONE THING.

And finally, we take a brief look at how to share the love. Remember, learning is a team game: getting others involved helps them as much as it helps you. How has what you have worked on 'infected' (in a good way) others? By observing this, you'll be able to see how you can continue to encourage positive change in yourself and those around you.

»

These days you can't afford to wait for what you want to learn to be offered to you on a plate. You need to go out and get it. As you progress along your *iDevelop* journey, doing your ONE THING as part of *Project You* with the support of *The Team*, you will be learning how to learn. You may get deeper into something you already do and love, or you may be motivated to try learning something completely new. You may even find yourself influencing others to take their own learning journey. Ultimately, *iDevelop*'s aim is to help you stay curious about life and be constantly delighted to discover something unexpected.

I hope this journey will be positive, fruitful and a bit of a stretch for you ... more yoga, less rack. As David Peterson, director of executive coaching and leadership at Google says: 'Staying within your comfort zone is a good way to prepare for today, but it's a terrible way to prepare for tomorrow.'[1]

Remember that everyone, everywhere, everyday is learning. It's time for you to recognise how you do it too, and to do it consciously.

Now ... let's get started!

The *iDevelop* Journey

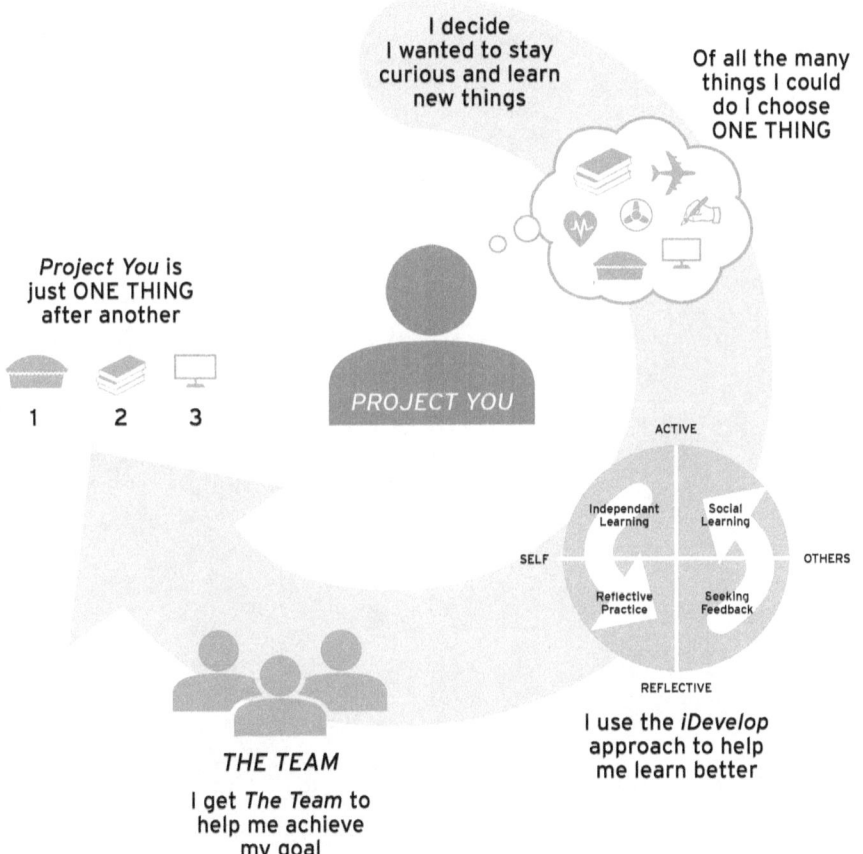

CHAPTER 1
WHY LEARNING MATTERS NOW

The single biggest driver of business impact is the strength of an organization's learning culture.

JOSH BERSIN[2]

In many organisations, professional development has been shifting from a predominantly set menu, where there are limited or no options about what, how and when we learn, to a more a-la-carte approach that has a range of learning dishes to choose from. But now even this isn't enough. According to Gallup: 'Today's workplaces evolve too rapidly and are too complex to offer nothing more than how-to learning experiences.'[3]

There is a growing recognition that it's time we let people cook for themselves by stocking the kitchen with ingredients that nourish development, and then supporting them in giving things a go.

> *Rather than focusing on knowledge and skills, organizations need to equip employees with mindsets that encourage their success. It's the difference between telling employees what to do and teaching employees how to think.*[4]

However, continuing the food metaphor just a little longer, there are still organisations where the cupboard remains bare and people simply go without, often for what appear to be immovable reasons: the company is small, the people are not interested, time off for development is too difficult to schedule, there is nothing out there which is all that relevant to the business.

Bearing this in mind, part of *Project You* will involve re-tooling your approach to learning. In order to develop your skills and ability to learn more naturally, let's first focus on The Big Five of Learning: curiosity, clarity, commitment, content and connection.

The Big Five of Learning

Curiousity	Clarity	Commitment	Content	Connection
Discover how you work, how you learn, and what really matters to you	Decide and focus on the ONE THING you really want to learn right now	Know what keeps you from changing, build strong habits and measure key moments	Tap into our resource-rich world of information and find what's valuable for you	Involve others to support you, hold you accountable and see you a little differently

1. Curiosity
Discover how you work, how you learn, and what really matters to you.

Being curious about ourselves, those around us and how the world works usually comes naturally to us, but too often a fixed mindset and/or unconscious biases can distort our understanding of what we see and learn. Fostering a curiosity about strategies and processes that can help you reflect on your actions is a necessary first step to identifying what is really going to make a difference to your learning. This knowledge, along with an understanding of the different ways people learn, can help you become the best you can possibly be, as well as helping you interpret the actions of others more easily.

2. Clarity
Decide and focus on the ONE THING you really want to learn right now.

Some folk find making decisions almost impossible. Too much choice can be paralysing. Trying to do too many things at once is exhausting, confusing and undermines quality outcomes. So, when it comes to learning, we need to focus on ONE THING at a time. Gaining clarity on what that ONE THING will be may require some self-reflection and feedback from others. You might need to make sure that your ONE THING is a good size – not too big, not too small – so that it won't overwhelm or bore you. It's not always easy deciding on ONE THING, but you do have to decide. Even if your choice is not the exact right, best ever, most important single thing you could do, your first ONE THING will still be good enough for you to learn more about yourself and what is important to you. Then you can do that other ONE THING next.

3. Commitment

Know what keeps you from changing, build strong habits and measure key moments.

Once a commitment is made and action is taken, there are things that supercharge progress and things that can get in the way. Gaining an understanding of any barriers you may have can help identify how to build a bridge and get over them. We know that remaining committed to a course of action can't just rely on willpower (a very scarce resource!). Knowing how to build great habits through some simple hacks will help sustain your commitment to your goals. While the final outcome is important, identifying the key milestones as you progress allows you to celebrate along the way. This can really propel you forward to the next step in your learning.

4. Content

Tap into our resource-rich world of information and find what's valuable for you.

Ever walk into a supermarket and think, *Where did all this stuff come from?* Much like our dietary environment, our knowledge environment is brimming with abundance. It's easy to get overwhelmed by variety and choice and, unfortunately, not all of this information is nutritious. Finding content is easy. Being able to identify whether it is quality content and good for our health, or simply junk food for the brain, can be more difficult. As you learn how to research and discover the content that works for you, you'll find that there are many free or inexpensive options for learning. And remember, not all of it comes from books, MOOCS (Massive

Open Online Courses), workshops, conferences or online learning – some great opportunities come from trying stuff out, self-observation and listening to others.

5. Connections
Involve others to support you, hold you accountable and see you a little differently.

Learning is not a spectator sport; it's a team sport and most people want to master their position in the game. Getting others on board with what you are doing is an important part of *Project You*. Not just any 'others' though; they need to be a blend of cheerleader – ready to celebrate your achievements – and tough, yet compassionate coach – someone who will call you on your BS, but in a nice way. Plus, these people who are not you often have some great ideas and novel perspectives that could help you succeed. Bear in mind, there will also be a few well-intentioned, less-than-useful ideas offered, but generally, creating strong connections with supportive people will be hugely beneficial to you and your learning journey. We'll be talking about how to build this personal support group – aka, *The Team* – a little later in this book.

The future

We hear a lot about the rapid pace of change, the ubiquity of digital disruption, our VUCA (volatile, uncertain, complex and ambiguous) world and the need to adapt or die. Just thinking about it exhausts me! I've been around long enough to have heard more than once that the world of work will be changing soon. Like Christmas or birthdays, which you can't ever imagine not looking forward to when you are young, hearing something repeatedly starts to get … dull? Maybe a little old? Certainly a little obvious. It seems as if lots of very smart people like to tell us about what we need to be doing as organisations and as individuals to survive or thrive. But all we can be sure about are three things – we don't know with certainty what will happen, we can't know exactly what we will need to deal with it, and that we will undoubtedly need to be ready.

Anyone working today is likely to have heard that in this new workscape we need to be adaptive, flexible and nimble. Who would argue with that? Who sees themselves as maladaptive, inflexible and ungainly? Maybe you've met this person at work, but it's not you.

To deal with this lack of certainty, there is an emerging need to be ready for anything, anytime. At a basic level, understanding how we think, how we learn and how we treat other people seems like a good place to start in order to become adaptive, flexible and nimble. These highly prized and bendy sounding attributes are a way of thinking and working that occur in a specific context. You can't directly teach them, but they can be learned – and you learn them by being adaptable, flexible and quick thinking *in the moment of execution.*

And that is the purpose of this book. It gives you autonomy to learn these things as you develop what you need right now. It's a twofer. By identifying something you need to learn, turning it into a project where you can discover more about how to learn, think and engage with others, you will be ready with what you need now and ready for whatever comes next.

As natural as breathing

Most babies are like scientists. They are constantly observing and testing things out and getting feedback on what's working. The stimulus of the strange new things they encounter – and everything is strange and new to a baby – makes lots of lovely connections in the brain and, *voila!* Learning happens. For them, it's as natural as breathing. As adults, it doesn't always feel so easy.

> *One of the most obvious but striking things about a modern education is that you go through it only once. You show up every day for a number of years, get filled up with knowledge and then, once you're twenty-one or so, you stop – and begin the rest of your life.*[5]

Perhaps this observation isn't as true as it once was, but we still tend to front-load formal learning and conflate learning with education. The formal education system schools us until young adulthood, and then we are expected to head out into the so-called 'real world' of work – a horrid expression that diminishes the realities of all those people who aren't involved in paid employment, such as students, stay-at-home parents, children, job seekers, the elderly or the infirm.

It's now much more common for people to return to formal education at some point, either to the university or TAFE sectors. Mature-age students are taking advantage of the flexibility that studying online offers them and are able to attain degrees or qualifications while working. This means that even the traditional avenues of education can be spread more broadly across our lifetime. And, for a small number of professions in Australia, Continuing Professional Development (CPD) is an annual requirement in order to remain accredited to practice.

Yet there still needs to be a bigger picture to learning, besides formal education, that encompasses all the ways we gain new knowledge and skills throughout our lives. Most large Australian organisations address employee learning in a range of modes, but this may not always be done in ways that are well targeted, uniformly accessible or effective. There is still debate on, and continuing development in, how this can be best achieved. What we do know is:

> *The future of work will be more nimble, complex, digital and collaborative than ever before. For employees, the demands of this future environment will be considerable and constantly changing. Consequently, if leaders don't change the way they approach development, they cannot expect sustained performance excellence.*[6]

If this is the case, continuing to separate the ideas of 'work' and 'learning' seems strange and absurd. Learning is a fundamental component of work. So, until more organisations reconnect learning with work, we will need to be responsible for ensuring our own continuing development.

Like those scientist babies, everything we perceive and experience in our world shapes us. Some of it we notice and use in some way; some of it enters our subconscious. We exist in a sea of information that continually shapes who we are – especially at work. Therefore, we need to become more aware of what we are learning from the people, experiences and the information we engage with. We need to use what we know to become the best version of ourselves, and to build a stimulating career and fulfilling life.

> *Watch your thoughts, for they become words;*
> *Watch your words, for they become actions;*
> *Watch your actions, for they become habits;*
> *Watch your habits, for they become character;*
> *Watch your character, for it becomes your destiny.*
>
> **UNKNOWN**

This brings us back to *Project You*. To make this happen, to take control of your continual development, and to realise that learning can again become as natural as breathing, you'll need to understand some key points about how we learn.

Let's take a look at these next.

CHAPTER 2
LEARNING 101

If you are not willing to learn, no one can help you.
If you are determined to learn, no one can stop you.

ZIG ZIGLAR

How would you describe your relationship to professional development, to learning new things and acquiring additional skills? For myself, it's a bit like how I think about romance: it's either a fantasy, a fling or a forever kind of thing.

When I hear someone playing a beautiful melody on a piano I might think, *I so want to be able to do that.* When I see a leader authentically deliver a message that traverses the line between strength and compassion, I think, *Wow! I want to learn how to be that strong and kind and present.* I lust after the feeling of being able to create that or be that. I imagine how great that would be and what I would need to do to make it happen. And it might stop right there. That's my fantasy learning experience.

Or maybe I get a keyboard and download some things off the internet and try to figure out what I need to do to learn this one piece. After a few months, weeks, days, hours or minutes, I stop doing the work and put the keyboard in the garage or sell it on eBay. Or I read a book on authentic leadership and talk to a couple of people about it, but then get busy again. That's a learning fling. We had some fun. Made a bit of music. But that's it. Kiss, kiss, bye-bye.

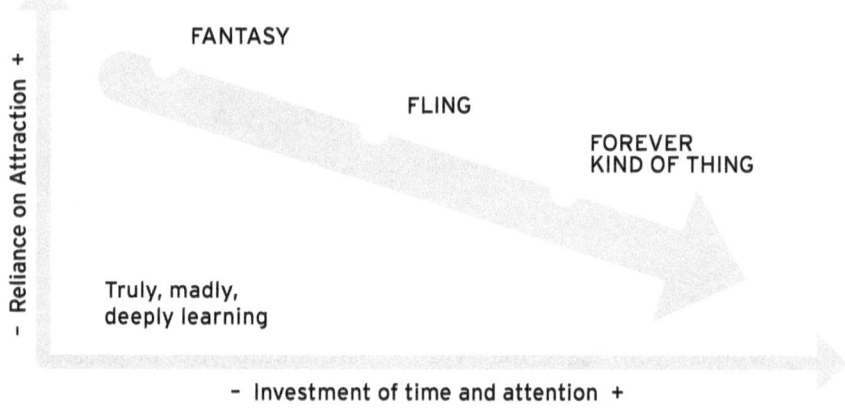

The Learning Relationship

If I remember my fling fondly for a few moments every now and again, it slips back into fantasy – and sometimes embarrassment or regret. But if I have the desire to continue and am prepared to do the work necessary, the relationship starts to become more serious, and soon it's turning into a forever kind of thing. That's a love connection.

If I am not so committed but I do the work anyway, I could eventually come to love what I'm working on and it could still become a forever kind of thing. That's successful matchmaking. Either way, like any forever kind of relationship, you must do the work and you must do it every day. Not every day is easy, but not every day is hard. And don't forget that there will be plenty of fun and fulfilling times that will make the journey fabulous and rewarding.

Some helpful ideas about learning

There are a lot of theories about how we learn. Sorting through these can be confusing – and we don't need that. *Actually, I hear you asking, do we need to know any of this theory stuff?* You know I'm going to say 'yes' because I have included it here. That's because I honestly believe having a general grasp of how we learn can help to inform our approach. It can highlight reasons why some of the ways we have gone about learning before haven't really worked, and can offer guidance to help us become more successful and effective learners in the future.

As this book is more of a 'how to' than a theoretical text, the following are brief summaries of some influential ideas about how we learn. Having at least a basic grasp of these is likely to help make your efforts at any future learning become more efficient and lasting. You may find some of these theories and models are more useful to you than others, but together they'll give you an overview of some very helpful things about learning in general.

There are six ideas or models that make up our picture of how we learn. The first looks at the importance of our beliefs about our capacity to learn by examining the concepts of fixed mindset (where people believe that intelligence is inherent and immutable), and growth mindset (where people believe that it is possible to master skills and enjoy challenging themselves). The second acknowledges that learning requires effort and outlines some predictable signposts and responses on the path to mastery.

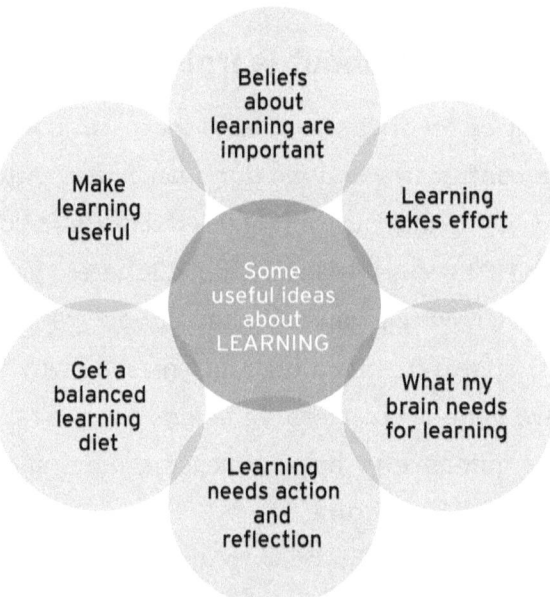

Key Learning Theories

The next model examines findings from neuroscience that acknowledge how our brains are wired to learn and what it takes to make learning more brain-friendly and efficient. Then we look at how both action and reflection play a key role in how we learn, and at the different ways and modes we can use to learn, with a particular focus on the 70:20:10 model. Finally, we look at ensuring learning is applied where it is most needed and is transferred to our workplace practices and behaviours.

Mindset matters: how our beliefs support our learning

One of the most pervasive and interesting ideas about how we learn originates from the work of psychologist Carol Dweck, and relates to the distinction between fixed and growth mindsets. Someone with a fixed mindset looks at intelligence as something that people are born with and is static. If a person has been blessed with great genetics or some kind of natural talent, then they're very lucky. If not, then there is nothing to be done. People with a fixed mindset tend to think, *If it's not something in my control, how would learning benefit me and why would I do it?*

Someone with a growth mindset believes that intelligence can be developed through effort. You can see how a growth mindset would mean someone would be much more likely to engage in learning and prioritise their development.

The following table outlines the key characteristics of fixed and growth mindsets:

PEOPLE WITH A FIXED MINDSET	PEOPLE WITH A GROWTH MINDSET
Believe intelligence is static	Believe intelligence can be developed
Want to appear smart	Have a desire to learn
Avoid challenges	Embrace challenges
Give up when faced with obstacles	Persist regardless of obstacles
Believe that effort is pointless because intelligence is fixed	Believe that making the effort is how we master something
Ignore feedback	Learn from the feedback of others
See the success of others as threatening	Are inspired by the success of others

By believing there is only a finite amount of ability or intelligence in the world, people who have a fixed mindset often feel insecure and want to hang on to the information they have, rather than share it. They are likely to think there is no point to learning, or getting feedback from others, because they believe there is nothing they can do to improve their skills and knowledge.

Someone with a growth mindset is more generous with what they know. They don't feel threatened by knowledge that others have because in their mind, knowledge and skills are out there for everyone to learn. This makes them more comfortable with taking risks and trying difficult things, because they know that people continue to develop by doing so.

It's pretty clear how different these two mindsets are, and how understandable the conclusions that people with either mindset draw from their core beliefs. While we don't have the space here to go into detail about where these beliefs may have come from, know that *iDevelop* has a growth-mindset approach baked in. Plus, I would hazard a guess that if you are reading this book, a fixed mindset is not a big issue for you. It can be situational though, and you may uncover evidence of fixed-mindset thinking in some particular aspects of your life. If there are situations where you would like to loosen a fixed mindset (whether that's yours or those of others), you could consider having that as a focus for a future ONE THING as you continue your work on *Project You*.

QUESTIONS TO CONSIDER
» Would you describe yourself as having a fixed mindset or growth mindset?
» Are there situations where you demonstrate aspects of the opposite mindset?
» Can you identify aspects of a fixed mindset or a growth mindset in colleagues at your workplace?

Effortful to effortless: the stages of learning

Learning a new skill, process or behaviour is going to take some hard work, but there are a few things we can do to make it less effortful (because it won't be effortless!) and make it stick.

This brings us to the 'conscious competence' model that describes the journey to mastery, or how to make something you learn more 'automatic'. This is especially helpful because of how our brain handles new information. Turns out, learning new stuff is exhausting. The brain uses a lot of fuel when it's learning, but once something is automated it is stored in a different part of the brain

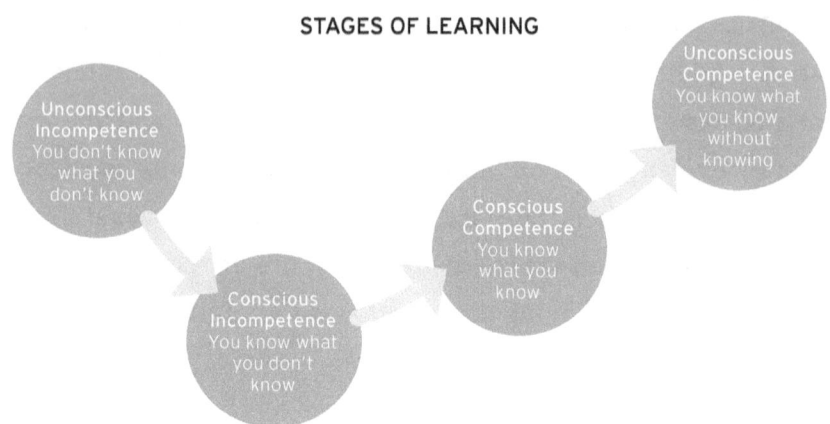

Conscious Competence Learning Model

and becomes effortless. Let's use the example of learning how to drive to demonstrate exactly how this works.

One day I was spending time with a friend and her seven-year-old son, who was asking when he could start driving. She asked him when he thought he should and he was confident that he could do it straight away, "coz it doesn't look that hard. I steer really well on my video game.' With most things, we start out feeling okay about what we want to learn. Like my friend's son, we tend to overestimate our abilities ... until we try. This is the 'unconscious incompetence' stage, when you don't know what you don't know.

Things go downhill a little after this as we quickly enter the 'conscious incompetence' stage, and become all too aware of the things we are yet to master. This bit is crucial. People can get so discouraged at this point that they give up. Don't do that! I learnt to drive in a manual car in a very hilly country town. For me, becoming competent at hill starts (getting the handbrake, gears and accelerator synchronised as you start the car so you don't stall or kangaroo hop ... or roll back down the hill) and reverse parking was a nightmare. I thought I'd never get it right. Yet, if we force ourselves to continue, and we practice (like I did), we start to get okay at things (less kangaroo hopping, no stalling).

The next stage of learning is 'conscious competence' and it's still a bit bumpy. You can drive, but you are aware of a million things going through your brain. You have to remember to look in the mirror, put your seat belt on, depress the clutch and slowly engage the accelerator – oops, handbrake – and you're not even on the road yet, where you'll need to recall road rules, think about where you are going and look out for other people doing weird and unexpected things.

For those who drive regularly, it's easy to forget how much goes into the act of driving. Perhaps, like me, there are days when you are driving a familiar route and think, *I don't remember taking that turn near the river*. This means you have become 'unconsciously competent' in the skill of driving. It has become effortless, routine – you've mastered it. It no longer takes all your energy, which means that you now have energy for other things. Yeah! So it's easy to see that mastering things that you need to do frequently is a good investment, even if it takes some effort at the start.

You can also think about this model from another perspective, which can explain why showing someone else how to do something that's become second nature to you is hard work. Has that happened to you? When I have already automated a skill, explaining it to someone else feels like pulling all that knowledge through a very small aperture from the back of my brain to the front with a tiny hook in order to reconstruct how I learnt it. Only then can I share it with others. So exhausting!

QUESTIONS TO CONSIDER

» Think of something you do automatically. Can you identify how you moved through each stage on your way to mastering it?

» What was it like for you at each stage?

Using your brain: how the grey matter in your head likes to learn

I read somewhere (this means I can't find the source – so don't take it as gospel) that by putting an image of a brain into a presentation, the status of the information you are presenting is increased and is more readily believed. It seems that anything to do with the brain, and especially with neuroscience, is sexy right now. The information coming from this relatively new area of science is completely changing how we think about how we think. Funnily enough, sometimes it's telling us stuff that other areas of science or practice have been saying for a while ... it's just that now we also know which part of the brain 'lights up' when we think about or do particular things (learning included).

Don't get me wrong – I'm a huge fan of this stuff. So much of what is being discovered is helpful for how we think, learn, behave and understand our relationships. Understanding how the brain encodes information can really make what we are learning more 'sticky'. One very cool model that highlights how our brains learn is the AGES model,[7] developed by the NeuroLeadership Institute. AGES is an acronym for attention, generation, emotion and spacing. Knowing how they work together can help shape your approach to learning and increase the effectiveness of your efforts – and who doesn't want that?

The first aspect of the model, 'attention', is pretty obvious. Basically, being in a state that encourages good learning 'involves paying close attention to something relevant and interesting, with enough of a challenge to keep our attention'.[8]

The idea of 'generation' is a little more abstract. It refers to how we combine new information with information we already have, and put it into the context of our own experiences. This means people activate what they know from their individual circumstance and 'map new learning to their existing knowledge and experiences and generate their own meaning and ways to apply the new knowledge'.[9]

The AGES model highlights how 'emotion' plays an integral part in retaining what we learn. Knowledge embeds in the mind more deeply when we engage our emotions in learning – basically, we learn better when 'emotion' is part of the process. The great thing here is that learning doesn't have to be serious. Play lightly with your learning and be creative. Make it fun, make it rude (privately), make yourself laugh, make it a game. You are more likely to impede your ability to learn if you are anxious, sad or stressed out, so have fun with it instead.

While you might be having fun while you learn, it's important to remember that when you are learning a new thing, your brain gets exhausted quickly. The final strategy in this approach to brain-friendly learning is to pace yourself as 'spacing information over time leads to higher retrieval rates of new information and seems to build stronger long-term memory'.[10]

'Spacing' allows your brain to absorb the information you are feeding it. Don't try to do your learning all in one go. Don't do it only once. Give yourself time to think things through and go back over what you learn to help make it 'sticky'.

If we take the components of the AGES model into consideration, a good guideline to helping your brain learn goes something like this: focus your attention, make it meaningful to you, engage positive emotions to make it fun, and don't try to do it all at once. If you give these steps a go, you'll be working in line with, rather than against, how your brain likes to function.

QUESTIONS TO CONSIDER

» What is it that makes you focused or unfocused when you are learning something new?
» How could you make what you are learning more relevant to you?
» What creative things have you seen or done to make learning more interesting and a bit more fun?
» How might you better space what you're learning?

An agile learning practice: the importance of reflection and action

Educational theorist David Kolb's helpful model of experiential learning[11] points to the fact that we learn through a cycle of acting and reflecting on experience. We'll go into this point in more detail in the next chapter, but let's first take a look at the four stages of Kolb's process.

CONCRETE EXPERIENCE
Doing or having an experience

REFLECTIVE OBSERVATION
Reviewing and reflecting on the experience

ABSTRACT CONCEPTUALISATION
Drawing conclusions and learning from the experience

ACTIVE EXPERIMENTATION
Planning and trying out what you've learned

Kolb's Experiential Learning Cycle

His theory suggests that learning starts with a 'concrete experience'; that is, doing something – an action, a behaviour or a task. According to Kolb, you can't learn by simply watching or reading about something. To learn effectively, you must *do* something. One of the keys to learning is active involvement.

Stage two is 'reflective observation'. This is where you give yourself time to stop doing and instead, step back from the task to review what happened. Reflection then allows for the next step, 'abstract conceptualisation', to occur. This is the process of making sense of what has happened. What do you understand about the process and outcome?

These steps enable the fourth and final stage of the cycle, 'active experimentation', to take place. This is where you use your new understanding to make a plan before giving it a go. Then the cycle can start all over again.

Simple active and reflective practices are important to ensure a balanced approach to your learning, and will help to make your learning faster. That's why they are part of *iDevelop* and built into the structure of *Project You*. There'll be some great ideas about using these to best advantage in chapter 3.

QUESTIONS TO CONSIDER

- When you are actively trying to learn something new or change something old, how could you make some time for reflection?
- Do you feel you are more likely to err on the side of caution, sometimes spilling over into inaction? Or do you tend charge in?
- How do you go about applying lessons you learn as you develop?
- How comfortable are you with understanding and experimenting with new approaches based on what you have learned?

A balanced learning diet: different ways to learn

As you can see, there are a number of ways of looking at learning. You may be familiar with the 70:20:10 model already as it is used in quite a lot of organisations. In the 1980s, a US non-profit educational institution, the Center for Creative Leadership, created the 70:20:10 model for adult learning. The numbers represent the optimal proportions of 'experience', 'exposure' and 'education' for adults to learn successfully. There is some debate about the accuracy of the percentages, whether or not they are too theoretical, and the accuracy of how they are measured. But what matters to us right here, right now, is that this model helps us broaden our concept of how we learn.

The '70' in the model, 'experience', indicates that we learn most effectively by doing. It refers to the 'experiential learning' that happens during the flow of work, and how the opportunities to practise frequently and in situ more thoroughly embed learning. This 'experience' category refers to on-the-job tasks, activities and problem solving.

The '20' in the model, 'exposure', refers to 'relational' or 'social learning' – or, more simply, learning from others. The importance of this kind of learning is increasingly coming to the forefront of learning practice. Some of the ways we learn from others is through feedback, mentoring and coaching, as well as via professional, work and learning networks.

The '10' in the model, 'education', refers to 'formal learning' interventions. This is often what we automatically think about when we think of learning. Formal learning occurs in a classroom, workshop or online, and usually involves specifically designed programs. It may lead to some form of accreditation, but not always. Reading is also included in this category.

The 70:20:10 model shows us a broader concept of how we learn. It helps us to understand that we learn by doing, that we need good information, and that we learn better with the support and encouragement of others. Too often, individuals and organisations default to running a workshop or doing a course. The world of learning is much more than this. That is what the 70:20:10 model reminds us and it's also why I've written this book! I want to help you discover more of what's on offer.

QUESTIONS TO CONSIDER
- How well do you use different forms of learning?
- Do you have a general preference for 'experience', 'exposure' or 'education'?
- Which other form could you include more of to improve your learning?

Make learning useful: how to apply what you know

Professional development is only useful when it is taken out of the 'workshop' and into the workplace. To do this well, you will need three things – confidence in your ability to understand and embed what you learn; commitment to trying; and support from others, especially your managers and peers.

Now, confidence is a funny thing. As philosopher Eric Hoffer has been quoted as saying: 'To learn, you need a certain degree of confidence, not too much and not too little. If you have too little confidence, you will think you can't learn. If you have too much, you will think you don't have to learn.'

However, the following quote by marketing chief Amy Chan, from her book, *Battle Hymn of the Tiger Mother*, is also true: 'There's

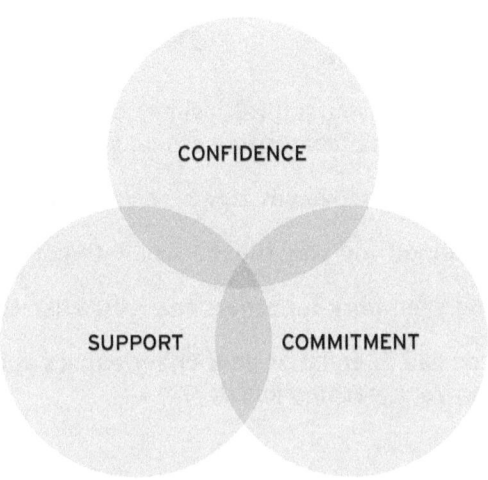

Transfer of Learning Model

nothing better for building confidence than learning you can do something you thought you couldn't.'

Going into learning, you need enough self-confidence to try something new. That's where commitment steps in. It takes commitment to learn something deeply enough so you can emerge confident at the other end. Confidence and commitment create a circle that can be virtuous or vicious. It helps to have the autonomy to decide what to learn – if it's meaningful to you, you are more likely to be committed to learning, even if it's a bit tough. And perhaps even more importantly, we need support because learning is a journey best taken together. We need others to help us as we embed the new things we are learning; to test us and keep us accountable; and to come to know us anew.

QUESTIONS TO CONSIDER

» How would you score yourself (10 = super-confident, 0 = not confident at all) when it comes to learning something new?

» What would it take to move you to where you want to be?

» What factors helped you stay the journey in the past?

» What have you seen work for others that you'd like to try?

» Who would you like to enlist as your cheerleaders and friendly challengers on your learning journey?

Why you should care

Each of these briefly described theories can help frame our approach to learning effectively. If we fail to believe that change is possible, that talent is only given to us by God or inherited through genes, there is no good reason to try to learn. However, the short outline this book provides on the importance of developing a growth mindset betrays the deeper change that Carol Dweck is concerned with. She says:

> *Mindset change is not about picking up a few pointers here and there. It's about seeing things in a new way. When people – couples, coaches and athletes, managers and workers, parents and children, teachers and students – change to a growth mindset, they change from a judge-and-be-judged framework to a learn-and-help-learn framework. Their commitment is to growth, and growth takes plenty of time, effort, and mutual support to achieve and maintain.*[12]

Self-directed learners already believe this. As Dweck says, it doesn't mean that learning is effortless. Becoming *consciously competent* (you know what you know), and then *unconsciously competent* (you know what you know without knowing) at the ONE THING you most want to learn is still a journey.

For optimal learning, our brains require us to be focused (attention); be invested in making learning relevant to our own situation and experiences (generation); engage our emotions to deeply embed what we learn (emotion); and to learn over time (spacing).

If we engage ourselves in a virtuous cycle of learning through reflective and active practice using different methods – from formal education (10), learning through others (20), and learning on-the-job (70) – we can build our confidence and commitment, and find the support to achieve our goals.

Most of these methods are covered throughout *iDevelop*, and in an accessible and practical way. And these important theories on learning are built into how we approach *Project You*.

So let's keep going.

CHAPTER 3
THE DYNAMICS OF LEARNING

Follow effective action with quiet reflection.
From the quiet reflection, will come even more effective action.

PETER DRUCKER

By now, you're probably getting the picture that your learning is your responsibility and it's important that you stay curious in order to reach your professional and personal goals. Remember, learning can happen anywhere. Not just in the classroom or in workshops, but anywhere. It's just a case of being open to it when it happens.

A very dear friend of mine, we'll call him Allan because that was his name, told me a story of how one of the most important decisions he made in his life was based on something he learnt from watching a dog take a wee on a lamppost. At the time of the incident, Allan was mid-career, successful and working as an executive in a multinational company. He had a beautiful architect-designed home, a wonderful wife and two great children. He wasn't unhappy, but he was feeling a little … troubled. He found it difficult to put his finger on the problem.

One day as he was driving to work in his sporty red car ('Yes,' he told me, 'I was a cliché.'), he got stuck in traffic. As he waited for the cars to start moving, he observed a little dog. It was small and a bit scruffy. The dog was strutting along the path and stopped to sniff a lamppost. Then the dog did a very strange thing. It started backing itself up the lamppost so that its hind legs were higher up the post than they would usually be. When the dog was as high up the post as physically possible, it lifted its leg and did a wee. Job done, it jumped down onto the ground again and happily trotted off.

Allan thought this was pretty odd behaviour. He drove on as the traffic started to clear but found himself reflecting on the episode. What had the dog been doing? Then he figured it out: the reason the dog went through that strange and uncomfortable looking manoeuvre was because it wanted its wee to be high up the post. It wanted the next dog that came along and sniffed the post to think that it, a scruffy little dog, was bigger than it actually was.

My friend felt a strong affinity with that dog. Turns out that the nagging feeling he had was about trying to be something he wasn't. Allan realised the discomfort he was experiencing, despite all the trappings of success, was due to his efforts in trying to impress the wrong people and making himself look bigger and more important than he actually was. The lesson he learnt from the dog that morning changed his life. He reprioritised what mattered, spent years retraining to become a university lecturer in a completely different field, and reinvigorated his love of creating art. He's retired from his job now but he's still an artist.

I love this story. If a man can learn an important lesson from watching a dog wee on a post it shows that with the right sort of awareness and reflection, we can learn anywhere and from anything. Any sort of change – and learning is change – arises from one of three places: chance, crisis, or choice. Allan's encounter with a scruffy pooch on a bad-traffic day was pure chance – but it led to a significant change for him. Aside from chance, the majority of us have had times when we've been forced to make changes, and usually not ones we want or like, because of a crisis of some kind. The only type of change we do have control over is the kind we choose. Staying curious and responsible for our continued development includes many things, but there are three key aspects we'll discuss now: the ability to reflect, take action and seek support from others. And that is our choice.

The model pictured on the following page is key to understanding our *iDevelop* approach and illustrates how we can make learning more dynamic and successful. The vertical axis represents a simplified version of Kolb's experiential learning model and looks at active and reflective learning. The intersecting horizontal axis demonstrates the role we play as individuals and how we engage with others in our learning. Let's examine this in more detail.

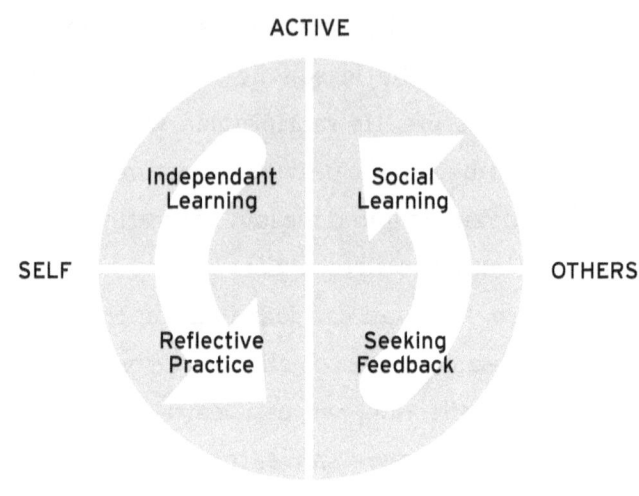

The *iDevelop* Learning Model

Reflective and active approaches to learning

People tend to have a preference for reflection or action as their primary approach to learning – or doing anything, really. Each has its own strengths and shortcomings. Those who favour reflection can sometimes get stuck in their heads and spend a lot of time figuring out the why and how and when of an idea or problem. Only after they have satisfied their thinking process do they prepare for action ... then they might think some more, maybe have a nap and then, finally, possibly take action. Now, as my dad told me when he was making things for our family home, it is wise to 'measure twice, cut once'. You can't uncut that too-short piece of wood. But when careful thought becomes over-thinking, it can turn into procrastination or paralysis.

Those who are more action-oriented like to get in and 'give it a go', preferring to figure out most things on the fly. This is brilliant for getting stuff done and, as an approach, seems to be currently in vogue: 'be agile', 'iterate'. This works in some instances but not in others. Sometimes 'Let's just give this a go' is seen as a replacement for thinking things through, and might not be a sound approach for high-risk or high-cost projects. You wouldn't want a manager trying out a different management style each week to see which one fits best, and you wouldn't want an engineer to just give it a go and see how those foundations hold, would you?

It seems obvious that combining reflective practice and active engagement is necessary. But you would be surprised how often reflection can take a back seat when people are trying to make decisions. For example, GROW[13] is a coaching model that structures a conversation around a task, issue or problem as follows: the 'goal' phase – deciding and becoming clear about what you are looking to solve; the 'reality' phase – thinking about all the information that may have an impact on your considerations (a form of reflection); the 'options' phase – using your understanding of the goal and the reality of the situation to come up with possible options for action (also reflection); and finally, the 'what's next' phase – or the 'action' part of the model, where you plan what you'll do to make things happen and do it.

It's a useful model but in my experience, whether working with groups or coaching individual clients, it's amazing how often people move from the goal phase straight to the what's next phase: 'Here is an issue, let's try this.' These are the action people. They want to solve the problem and are happy to go with their first thoughts. This can be problematic. If we don't think things through, we are prone to taking all sorts of cognitive shortcuts that may not serve us well. By thinking through a situation and its implications, we open up many more options and allow time for biases to surface.

However, in many cases, it won't actually matter where you start. Let's apply this to *Project You* and your ONE THING. If you have picked what you want to do, how did you go about it? If you haven't, how will you? If you are action focused, you could simply try something that isn't too costly, unsafe or time-consuming to begin with and then reflect on that; or if you prefer a bit of thinking first, you could spend some time (but not too much!) reflecting on how to proceed and then get going. The point is that reflection and action is a cyclical process; where you start will depend on the situation at hand. And remember: 'now' is nearly always the perfect time to reflect on your ONE THING so that you can kick off some action on *Project You*.

Independent and social learning

We have discussed the reasons why it's important to be accountable for your own ongoing development and touched on the need to not go it completely alone. These independent and social approaches integrate with our reflective and active practices. At the end of the day, and most of the other parts of the day as well for that matter, it will be you who has to put the work in. It is up to *you*. It's *your* ONE THING and *your Project You*. However, there are a few important reasons you'll want to get others involved in whatever you are hoping to achieve.

First, there are times when your reflections on your ONE THING may be ... how do I say this nicely ... less than fulsome? That's right, we all have blind spots around our behaviours and actions. It takes an external viewpoint to offer another perspective we might have overlooked. Secondly, it's also good to have others support your development because they can help hold you accountable to your goals – in a (mostly) nice way.

This is where *The Team* comes in. *The Team* is your own set of specifically chosen people who will support you through your learning phase. They function in a number of ways we'll look at later, but, in this context, they will help you see what you can't.

But there is another reason for getting others involved, especially if your ONE THING involves learning something that you hope will change how you behave and are perceived – or how you wish to behave and be perceived – because it's often more difficult to shift perceptions than reality.[14] Here's an example to explain what I mean.

Now, let's hope this is at the extreme end of the spectrum these days, but imagine you are a boss who has tended to be a bit shouty when people don't get things right. You have an epiphany about your behaviour and think, *This whole shouty thing is really the wrong way to treat my employees and colleagues. I am going to make a change.* So, you get some coaching, practice better ways to deal with your frustrations, learn to be more supportive and start listening to people more. It's possible that people around you will notice, but they have a lot going on and perhaps they lack a bit of awareness too. You are executing your new plan brilliantly until one day, eight months after you have started your new way of being, a series of unfortunate events – possibly not sleeping, a family or business crisis, feeling a little unwell – finds you not quite on top of your game. Something happens that tips you back into your shouty ways just once, just briefly. You even catch yourself quickly and apologise.

To those who are not aware of your efforts to make this behavioural change, you are – despite that long period of non-shouty-ness – still just the shouty boss. But if you discuss your intention to be less shouty with your peers and colleagues at the beginning, share how you think you will go about doing what is needed, and ask them what they think might work to help you, they will be on the lookout for changes in you. And, if they are willing to support your efforts by holding you to account, when you do slip up, you are perceived as a reformed shouty boss just having a bad day. If your peers and team members are aware of what you are doing, it will be much easier, and quicker, to recover their trust, and potentially use that bad-day experience for further growth.

To help you put these ideas into practice, we're now going to delve into understanding and developing your reflective practice. Then, in chapters 5 and 6, we'll follow this up with a look at how to take action, and how to identify the best ways to find support and involve others in your development so they will be fired up to help you achieve your ONE THING.

CHAPTER 4
REFLECTION

We do not learn from experience.
We learn from reflecting on experience.

JOHN DEWEY[15]

So what exactly is reflective practice and why is it important?

In a recent study, researchers examined what would be more predictive of future performance: 'individuals [who] seek to accumulate additional experience or ... [those who] focus on trying to articulate and codify the experience accumulated in the past?'[16] For example, should surgeons do ten more hours of practice, or reflect on the considerable amount of practice they already have and consolidate their learning? In confirmation of the John Dewey quote above, the researchers found 'deliberation to be a powerful mechanism behind learning'.[17]

Reflection isn't something new. We all reflect. Apparently, when your brain isn't doing anything else, such as focusing on a task, it switches on its 'default network', which spends its time reflecting. As the social psychologist Matthew D. Lieberman tells us, essentially, 'our brains are built to practice thinking about the social world and our place in it'.[18]

This is great news, because it means it's not just me who has a version of Aunt Doris and Aunt Edna in their heads (you'll get to meet them later). Every day, situations find a way of locking into our thoughts so we can rethink, explore and reconsider them. This is especially true if it's something that didn't go so well. (Plus, it tends to be a great activity for two o'clock in the morning, don't you find?) Most of us would prefer that the often trivial things we ruminate on would float away to where all the facts we don't need to recall go, rather than hanging around and taking up valuable time and energy. However, by taking our innate ability to reflect and giving it some focus as well as a little bit of structure, we can make reflection conscious and useful when we are actively trying to learn something new, like our ONE THING.

So, let's look at this more deeply. What is reflective practice? Linda Lawrence-Wilkes, an expert in the area, defines it as 'the use of self-analysis to understand, evaluate and interpret events and experiences in which we are involved'.[19] Reflection helps us develop insights into our own experiences and articulate them to others more easily. According to Lawrence-Wilkes, this learning aids 'new personal understanding, knowledge, and action, to enhance our self-development and our professional performance'.

Now, if reflection is something we do every day, what's the big deal here? I think Jennifer Porter, executive and team coach, sums it up nicely in her article addressed to business leaders (but which is applicable to everyone):

> The most useful reflection involves the conscious consideration and analysis of beliefs and actions for the purpose of learning. Reflection gives the brain an opportunity to pause amidst the chaos, untangle and sort through observations and experiences, consider multiple possible interpretations, and create meaning. This meaning becomes learning, which can then inform future mindsets and actions. For leaders, this 'meaning making' is crucial to their ongoing growth and development.[20]

How to develop a reflective practice

First, a caveat: the following is not a deep dive into mindfulness and how to create a life-long mindfulness practice. That is an important topic that you may wish to explore in the future, but it's not needed right here, right now, as we initially come to understand our *iDevelop* journey. What we'll be talking about is observing yourself in the process of learning, and using these reflections to be more successful in achieving your ONE THING and *Project You* goals.

Basically, this means we'll be talking about you thinking about your thinking.

How aware are you of the way you think? Can you recognise biases and assumptions you may have? This type of self-analysis is known as 'meta-cognition' – your analysis, understanding and awareness of your thought processes.

Dr David Rock, founder of the NeuroLeadership Institute, calls this awareness your 'Director'.[21] Understanding it this way can be a little less challenging for those who consider the concept of 'mindfulness' a bit 'woo-woo', or left of centre.

According to Dr Rock, your inner Director represents 'the part of your awareness that can stand outside of the experience' and is vital for learning. Without it you would have 'little ability to moderate and direct your behaviour moment-to-moment'. A director tells the actors and the audience where to focus their attention. In our context, your inner Director will keep you aligned with what really matters.

The following techniques will help you discover your inner Director and help you shape a reflective practice that will work for you.

Create a quiet environment

Ulrich Boser, founder of The Learning Agency, identifies a prerequisite for reflection as 'cognitive quiet'. He says:

> Learning benefits from reflection. This type of reflection requires a moment of calm. Maybe we're quietly writing an essay in a corner – or talking to ourselves as we're in the shower. But it usually takes a bit of cognitive quiet, a moment of silent introspection, for us to engage in any sort of focused deliberation ... The idea of cognitive quiet also helps explain why it's so difficult to gain skills when we're stressed or angry or lonely. When feelings surge through our brain, we can't deliberate and reflect.[22]

The question then is how will you create some time, space and calm to reflect as part of *Project You*? 'Oh No!' I hear you say. 'I am so busy already, plus I'm doing the Project thing and now I have to find more time? Seriously?' But it doesn't need to take much time. In fact, reflection can be incorporated into something you are already doing. I'm confident that as you read further, you will discover how to find the right fit for you.

In her book *How to Have a Good Day*,[23] Caroline Webb shares a quick reflective practice one of her clients does at the end of each day. Her client calls it a 'DATE'. She identifies something that she has *discovered* – perhaps an interesting idea, something she learnt or will do differently; reflects on what has been *achieved*; identifies something she is *thankful for*; and focuses on one specific thing she has *experienced* that day within work or beyond. Her client says it helps her see the significance of and value in each day, good or bad.

Below are a few other easy ways you could fit reflection into the routine of your day:

Walk it	On your morning run or walk, turn off the headphones and recap what you learnt from yesterday before focusing on the day ahead.
Rinse and repeat	As you lather up in the shower, find some focus. This is often quite a productive space. You might need to make some notes after, so don't forget to factor that time in too.
Caffeinate it	Make time to sit down somewhere quiet(ish) for a coffee and a think at the start of the day.
Meeting with me	You already have a lot of meetings, so why not set up a short daily meeting with yourself - at least you know that this one will be useful, and you will know why you're there!

Work it out	While you are working out at the gym on equipment that doesn't require too much concentration - on a treadmill, for example - allow yourself some headspace for reflection.
Car-park contemplation	Take five minutes in the car before you drive home from work to take a breath and reflect on the day that was. It's important to remind yourself that the people (or fur babies) waiting for you at home deserve your best you, and not cranky-pants-because-of-banal-office-politics you.
Sleepy time	Last thing before bed, take a little time to reflect and ... oh ... zzzzz ...

And remember: wherever and whenever you end up reflecting on things – especially your ONE THING – get yourself into a good frame of mind. Take a few deep breaths and approach it lightly. You are making time to learn something about yourself – learning means you don't have it down pat yet, so try not to be too hard on yourself.

Ask the right questions

The ways in which we ruminate on things that happen during the day are not always helpful. We can be griping about something or someone; letting ourselves off the hook by trying to be right rather than curious; being tough on ourselves rather than kind; and letting our biases diminish our objectivity. This might be because we are not asking ourselves helpful questions.

Turns out that 'Why' questions are not very productive.[24] If you've ever spent time with an inquisitive two-year-old child, you may know just how very annoying 'Why' can be. Quite often, we don't have a ready understanding of all our motivations, thoughts and feelings in a given situation. We tend to invent things to provide a rationale for why something happened. There is also a tendency to go to negative explanations that make us depressed or anxious about our performance or behaviours. For example, when we ask ourselves, 'Why did I get a poor performance rating?' it can spin us into self-incrimination or blame. When we ask our boss that question, it could come across as accusatory. A 'Why' question may not even have a definitive answer.

A more productive approach is to ask 'What' questions, such as, 'What reasons could there be for me not getting a similar rating as last year?' These types of questions tend to promote more constructive thinking and are often more helpful in the long run. You can practise turning your queries into 'What' questions with *The Team* when working on your ONE THING.

There are a few frameworks for questions that support reflective practice. One model[25] that is easy to call to mind as you reflect on an action asks the following:

- *What?* First ask what happened in the thing you are currently focused on (in our context, your ONE THING).
- *So What?* Think about what that means in terms of the outcome.
- *Now What?* Then consider what you could do differently next time.

Beautifully simple and a great place to start, right? However, watch out that you don't become a bit flippant with your responses. Just because it's a simple approach, doesn't mean there are simple answers. Also, it wouldn't hurt to add the word 'else' to each question after you respond the first time. What *else* did you notice

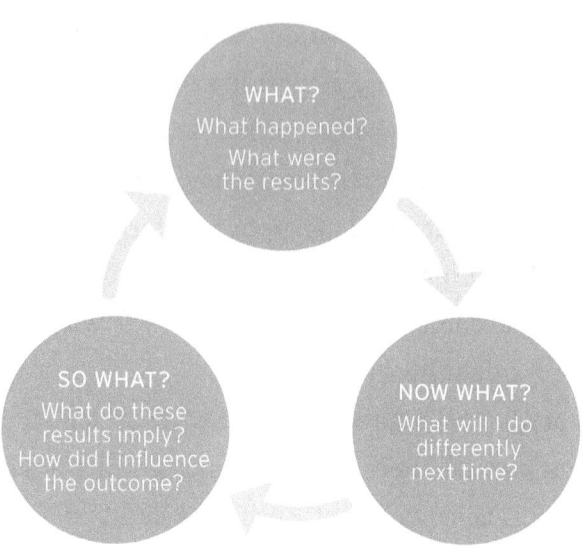

Rolfe's Reflective Model

happened; what *else* could that mean; and what *else* could you do differently? Doing this will take your reflective practice deeper and offer you more insight into *Project You* and your ONE THING.

Make a note

It's a great idea to make a note somewhere of things you decide on, or want to do, when thinking of your ONE THING. You can buy yourself a beautiful journal and handwrite your responses. You can draw a mind map, or go digital and type a task in the to-do list of your calendar. Maybe you have a special private journaling app that you can use on your phone. Or perhaps you might prefer something visual, like a photo journal, or something auditory, such as a voice recording. Whichever way you choose to record your responses and reflections, it doesn't need to be long or complicated. The key here is to use any insights you generate to enhance your learning. Keeping track of them makes the exercise more valuable. You can go back over them, see how far you've come, generate new ONE THINGs to work on, and be surprised by just how silly or brilliant that forgotten idea was.

Turn reflection into a habit

You can see how consciously taking time to reflect is going to speed your progress, but you need to make finding your quiet space to ask these simple but effective questions a routine. According to behavioural scientist Professor B.J. Fogg, a few key things to consider are that new habits are best to do in the morning, kept really small, and associated with something you are already doing.[26]

Building habits is a thriving area for research at the moment, providing some great practical advice. Check out *Atomic Habits* by James Clear, whose work we discuss elsewhere in this book. You might also like to consider these two pieces of advice I've found useful. First, habits are like compound interest, small changes make a very big difference over time. Secondly, the habit is the start of an action, not the achievement of the goal. So the habit you might build to become a marathon runner is putting on your running shoes and walking out the front door.

If you take these points into account, by keeping things small and manageable in your reflective practice you will be more likely to incorporate it into your daily routine.

The Next Step

So, we've reflected on reflection. We've learnt how to build and maintain a simple reflective practice that will help us throughout *Project You* and when deciding on that first ONE THING. We've done a lot of useful thinking and considering, and there'll be more to come.

But now, folks, it's time for action.

CHAPTER 5
ACTION

What we think or what we know or what we believe is, in the end, of little consequence. The only consequence is what we do.

JOHN RUSKIN[27]

I remember watching Oprah's show many years ago. One of the things she used to tell her guests after they shared an anguished story where they failed to do or be their best was: 'When you know better, you do better.' Certainly, this is good advice in many circumstances – to help stop people beating up on themselves when something doesn't turn out the way they expect, and certainly if they really didn't know any better. However, there is also this thing called the 'knowing-doing gap', which is when we do know better but choose not to go down that path. At times when watching that program, I felt that some of those guests really should have known and done better. Yes, sometimes I'm judgy.

Project You is about you doing better – and that will require action. Your ONE THING won't get settled on, or done, all by itself. A 2017 study found that while 97 per cent of people can readily identify a career-limiting habit, fewer than 10 per cent make substantial changes.[28]

So why is taking action and trying something new scary for some and exciting for others? We know that different learning preferences mean some of you will be finding the whole 'not doing something' challenging. That reflecting thing, just observing – yeah, that's hard. You have been waiting for this action bit! You are ready to just have a go at it. But then there are also natural over-thinkers (like me – guilty) who find lots of reasons to not do that thing. I know when I have a tidy house and the cat has stopped asking to be brushed, I've been procrastinating.

So, for those of us who might need a little extra push to get started, or a gentle hand on the shoulder to prevent them diving in the deep end, it might not hurt to get some balance here and think through the reasons why we feel like either running in or running away before we take action on our ONE THING.

When the overactive need to press 'pause'

Let's look at where you are in our *iDevelop* model. Out of the two 'active' quadrants at the top of the model, you don't need to worry

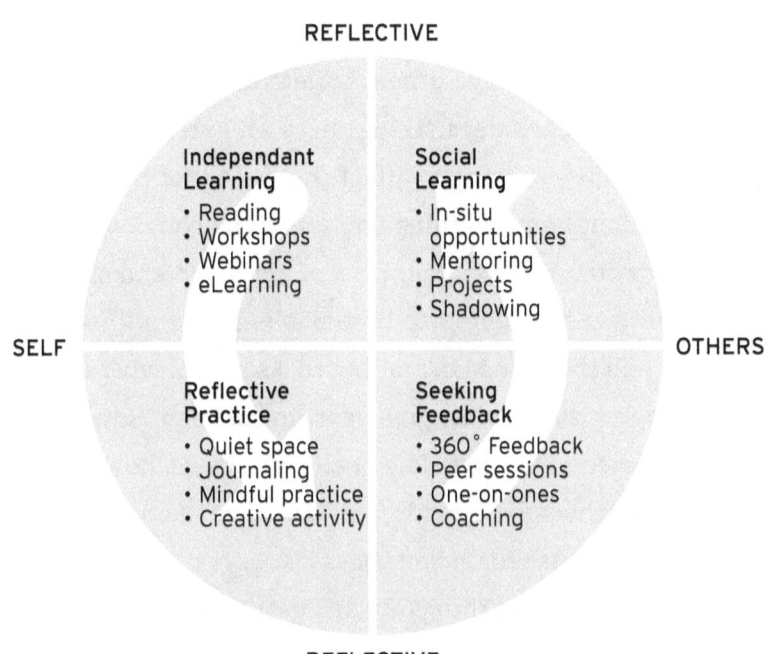

Examples for the *iDevelop* Learning Model

too much if you are looking at the 'independent learning' quadrant. Do as much learning as you like. The only word of caution here is to ensure that continued learning doesn't become a mechanism that prevents you from applying your learning to real-life situations, or stops you from reflecting on how it aligns with your purpose. Learning for learning's sake can be fun and addictive – but you need to make it meaningful as well.

If we move into the other active quadrant, the 'social learning' sphere, this means that others are involved too. This is where a little discretion needs to be shown to those who may not know that you are working on your ONE THING, or your *Project You*.

Where you can, involve others by letting them in on what you are trying to do. Consider making them an extension of *The Team* if your ONE THING is going to affect them. Ask for their help, what they think about how the thing you are doing could work, or what could work better. Discuss your plan of approach and ask for some feedback on it. Be prepared to be flexible. If you still want to try something and the group isn't on-board, ask them where or when it would be appropriate. This is great learning in itself. How vulnerable are you prepared to be, how do you engage others, how well do you listen so that others feel heard? Yes, lots of good stuff to reflect on here that you can use for *Project You*.

While you are testing things out and getting super active, don't be too literal. You are not setting up some kind of science experiment. It's not as if you need to break your team into groups and test out what happens when you: (1) apply punishments; (2) apply praise; (3) ignore them; and (4) do nothing and use your group as a control. And you don't need to try a new approach every day – Day 1: Apply 'command and control' leadership; Day 2: Apply 'coaching' leadership, etc. Okay, these examples are probably a bit extreme, but just remember, if others are involved, it might be a good idea to reflect a little before jumping into your experiment.

Keep in mind that although what we have discussed here may not be applicable for your current ONE THING, there will certainly be instances when a safety-first approach is best. And if you are keeping *The Team* involved in what you are doing, they will be a great sounding board for identifying when this might be.

When overthinkers need to press 'play'

If you are an over-thinker, this whole taking-action thing can be tricky. You are more comfortable erring on the side of caution – reading another article, making that plan a bit more fulsome, and checking the cat is super cosy. While I am a huge over-thinker, I'm with Kyle Eschenroeder, author of *The Overthinker's Guide for Taking Action*, when he says: 'I hate writing about taking action. I feel like an idiot. We already know we need to take action! Why talk about it?'[29] It is one of those incredibly obvious things, but sometimes we just don't. We can find seemingly endless reasons (excuses) to not do something. Nike's encouragement to 'Just Do It' isn't enough for us.

It's important to acknowledge that even when you have committed to a course of action, it might work out as you expect, or it might not. But that isn't a good reason not to try. If over-thinkers take this onboard, it will enable them to move towards action. Later in this chapter, we also take a look at how hidden beliefs can be a cause for inaction, but, in the meantime, let's see how over-thinkers (like myself) and everyone else can get moving.

Taking a leap of faith

Eschenroeder says he has two key tenets for taking action. The first is to always err on the side of action as long as the pain isn't irreversible. Susan Jeffers said something similar in her classic book *Fear the Fear and Do it Anyway*[30] – the clue is in the name. She wanted to acknowledge that the feeling of fear is part of the package and doesn't ever go away as you continue to grow. Everyone feels like this. Everyone. Especially that super-confident person you are pointing to right now (maybe just in your head). There is no point in waiting to be unafraid. In fact, the only way to overcome the fear is to take action. As Jeffers says, 'Pushing through fear is less frightening than living with the bigger underlying fear that comes from a feeling of helplessness!'[31]

When you are thinking about taking action that feels a little scary (and remember, it's often on the slightly scary edge where the good stuff happens) try reframing it in your mind as a leap of faith. Trust that the action will work out, but accept there are no guarantees. Be prepared to come out looking either 'golden' or 'a bit of goose'. It reminds me of the movie *Love Actually*. Sam, a young boy having missed the opportunity to tell the girl he loves how he feels, agrees to go to the airport to do just that. He says, 'Okay, Dad. Let's do it. Let's go get the shit kicked out of us by love.' (Just watch it!) You must be prepared to take a risk. The only sure way you can fail is not to act at all.

> *Sometimes your only available transportation is a leap of faith.*
>
> MARGARET SHEPARD

Building momentum

Newton's first law of motion states that 'an object at rest stays at rest and an object in motion will stay in motion until it meets a resisting force'.[32] Your first action, your leap of faith, begins to create momentum. As Tony Robbins says, 'The most important thing you can do to achieve your goals is to make sure that as soon as you set them, you immediately begin to create momentum.'[33] So, in the context of Project You, just take one step. One small step. Don't leave the room without taking that first, tiny step towards your ONE THING. And here is an important tip: be careful not to confuse doing ('action') with reading, planning or thinking about doing ('activity') – which can feel like action but isn't.

> *The best time to plant a tree was 20 years ago.*
> *The second-best time is now.*
>
> **CHINESE PROVERB**

Now here comes Eschenroeder's second tenet for taking action: act before researching. He says that this 'is not a rule against research'. It's just that usually we have collected quite a lot of knowledge through learning already and we often forgot to apply it to anything useful.[34]

I don't think he is suggesting doing brain surgery on a whim, or writing a whole book before you research anything, but he clearly states that you shouldn't prioritise reading a book (or several) on exercise, meditation, cooking or yoga before you exercise, meditate, cook something, or salute the sun a few times. Start creating the habit first. He reminds us, 'It's too tempting to try to sound smart instead of being effective ... and it's embarrassing how simple things actually are.' He quotes Warren Buffet reflecting on his success,

> *To the extent we have been successful, it is because we concentrated on identifying one-foot hurdles that we could step over rather than because we acquired any ability to clear seven-footers. The finding may seem unfair, but in both business and investments it is usually far more profitable to simply stick with the easy and obvious than it is to resolve the difficult.*[35]

Do something small and easily achievable to get a win on the board. Get your ONE THING ball rolling. And another thing, watch your language; don't 'should' all over yourself! You choose everything you do, so own that. Turn 'I really should do …' into 'I choose to do …' Our questions shape our answers, so rather than asking, 'What if I did …?', ask, 'How can I do …?'[36] It may seem like a little thing on the helping-to-build-momentum scale, but words do matter.

What's stopping you?

A friend of mine (his name is Allan but he's not the dog-and-lamppost guy), used to buy a TattsLotto ticket every week or two. He would buy the ticket and then put it in the back of the notes section of his wallet. One day, I was standing at the counter of a café as he was paying for coffee when I noticed he had quite a lot of TattsLotto tickets bulking up his wallet. I asked him if he had a problem and did we need to talk – or perhaps get him some help?

He assured me he wasn't a gambling addict and explained that he liked to buy the tickets and then think about what he would do if he won big. His dreams were the usual things – house, car, holiday, things his family and friends needed, and to leave his unsatisfying job. I asked him why he didn't check his tickets so he could find out about his fortunes. He said he rarely checked the tickets because he believed he would lose (which is not an irrational belief if you know the statistics for winning TattsLotto) and would rather hold on to the hope of winning than know he had lost.

When we learn something new, it will change us at some level. Our beliefs about what happens when we make this change can both spur us to action or hold us back. My friend wanted the change that winning a tub of money would bring, and would act enough to play, but never enough to realise the outcome. He would rather hope than act and potentially win. It's similar to going to a workshop, learning something life changing and then never using it. In their book *Immunity to Change*,[37] Robert Kegan and Lisa Lahey talk about this as having one foot on the gas and one on the brakes at the same time. We want to change or learn or achieve, but our underlying beliefs somehow hold us back.

Part of this reluctance is due to us projecting what the outcomes of trying something new will be and what this means for who we are or will become. Our fears can come from both our potential failure and our potential success. Like the proverbial iceberg, our beliefs can be hidden deep below the surface and not obvious to us. That can have an impact on our decisions around making the changes we want, following through on our goals, or it can keep us procrastinating. There are upsides and downsides to any change we decide to make – or not make. If we try to bring our beliefs to the surface, we can be more conscious of the decisions we make and the actions we take.

Let's face it, no one wants to feel or be considered unsuccessful. We'll all take looking golden over looking like a goose. Our beliefs around the consequences of doing something new, and changing who we are because of it, shape our actions. While we are more likely to be clear on the downsides that inhibit us acting, it is worthwhile to investigate the reasons why the upsides are also able to hold us back.

The upsides and downsides of learning motivation

Do you feel lucky?

There are times when the change we want to make or the thing we want to learn – maybe even your ONE THING – takes virtually no effort whatsoever. Without a skerrick of work or thought, it turns out we are great at this. While we can't rely on things falling into our laps, it's pretty cool when they do and we discover some kind of natural ability. It can, however, seem like this happens mostly to other people.

On the flipside, getting lucky in one area can foster a belief that we are great at everything and don't need to put in effort anywhere. For example, in business there is a common belief that a team member who is a technical expert is likely to be a good choice to manage a team. Or because someone is a good administrator, they are likely to be good in communications, event management or running a digital transformation project. These 'obvious' choices, however, can set people up to fail and come back to bite an organisation.

In some organisations, I have observed people progressing simply because they were still there and no one else was left. This can happen when there is a major restructure, or a significant change occurs to the leadership of a team or business. Suddenly those remaining are thrust into new roles without warning or a chance to prepare. I call this an 'Organisational Bradbury', after the Australian Olympic ice skater who won a gold medal when the rest of his competitors fell over. Some people thrive and step into their new role by assessing where they need to grow. Equally, others may experience the success of achieving a promotion only to fail in a role they did not recognise required new skills and some diligence in attaining them.

I can get some ... satisfaction

Succeeding at something that matters and that we've worked hard at … brilliant. It's obvious that experiencing success is a great driver and can spur us on; we all know how powerful the feeling of winning can be. We get addicted to the chemical hit our brain gives us when we win or successfully complete a task.

But success can also feel threatening. Being good at something can start to feel stressful if you believe you need to keep it up and always be doing better. Maybe you even feel a little like an imposter. This is very common. Sometimes you might encounter a voice in your head telling you that any minute someone is going to recognise you for the fraud you are and that everything has been a big mistake and you will have to leave. This sort of thinking can lead you to believe you should be in the 'lucky' quadrant of the model rather than being deserving of your achievements.

So perhaps play lightly with your successes and make sure your effort is leading to a more meaningful, better version of you. As Marianne Williamson's poem *Our Deepest Fear* expresses, we are more afraid of our power and our light, than our inadequacies or darkness. Playing small so others won't feel bad does not serve the world.[38] How you handle your successes and brilliance may just enable someone you haven't even met to feel more confident to shine.

I didn't do it my way

Regrets, we've all had a few, and hopefully too few to mention. People will avoid making changes in the belief that staying where they are is safe. If we fail to try to change, we shouldn't be surprised by the fact that we don't succeed. So, that's the upside – no surprises.

But not trying is a path to regret. It is a common aphorism that we don't regret what we have done, just what we didn't do when we had the chance – although that is only partially true. It is possible to regret things we do (a misspelt tattoo comes to mind). The fear of success can hold us back and leave our light firmly under that bushel. It can also leave us behind in the workplace. We can find ourselves one software upgrade or market disruption away from becoming redundant (not as people, but in what we thought was a secure job).

Remember, if you don't try, you will never know, and you may well live with that regret for some time.

Fail again, fail better

No one sets out to fail. It's also natural that you might feel like a bit of a goose if your efforts don't pay off. Just be careful not to stay disheartened for long – it's simply not helpful. Your mental state can suffer, and you could start to spiral into despair. In this state you can start to believe that this one failure defines you. It becomes who you are and will always be. Focusing on a failure is something many (probably all) of us do at some time. We can catastrophise an outcome to make it seem bigger and more permanent than it really is. If this happens to you and your feelings are preventing you from moving forward, seek help. Talk to someone on *The Team* or to a professional. Seeking help is the right step to take for you to move on.

Even if you fail at something that you have tried hard to make work, the upside is that you will have learnt something that will be useful – if not now, possibly in the future. Perhaps it has helped you count something 'in' or 'out' as an option. Maybe you gained a clearer view of the people who are there for you. You may even have figured out a little more about that enigmatic puzzle that is 'you'.

Amway has a saying for their sales people: 'Some will. Some won't. So what? Next.' If you are of a more literary bent, you might prefer Samuel Beckett's words, 'Ever tried. Ever failed. No matter. Try again. Fail again. Fail better.' It's often said, and it might even be true, the only failure is not trying.

DIY belief mapping

Belief mapping is a great way to identify what might be stopping you from learning or progressing your ONE THING. The model shown here will help you create a DIY belief map for your ONE THING or your *Project You*. Belief mapping can help you examine the beliefs that may contribute to your perceptions about change or learning something new. You can do this visually if you like with sticky-notes as shown, or draw them on your tablet – what-evs, just get them down.

Or for those who prefer to write a response in a journal or a notepad, you can use the questions outlined below.

» If I don't do my ONE THING and I still succeed I will feel/feel like a _____, and the upsides of that could be _____, while the downsides of that could be _____.

» If I do my ONE THING and I succeed I will feel/feel like a _____, and the upsides of that could be _____, while the downsides of that could be _____.

» If I don't do my ONE THING and I don't succeed I will feel/feel like a _____, and the upsides of that could be _____, while the downsides of that could be _____.

» If I do my ONE THING and I don't succeed I will feel/feel like a _____, and the upsides of that could be _____, while the downsides of that could be _____.

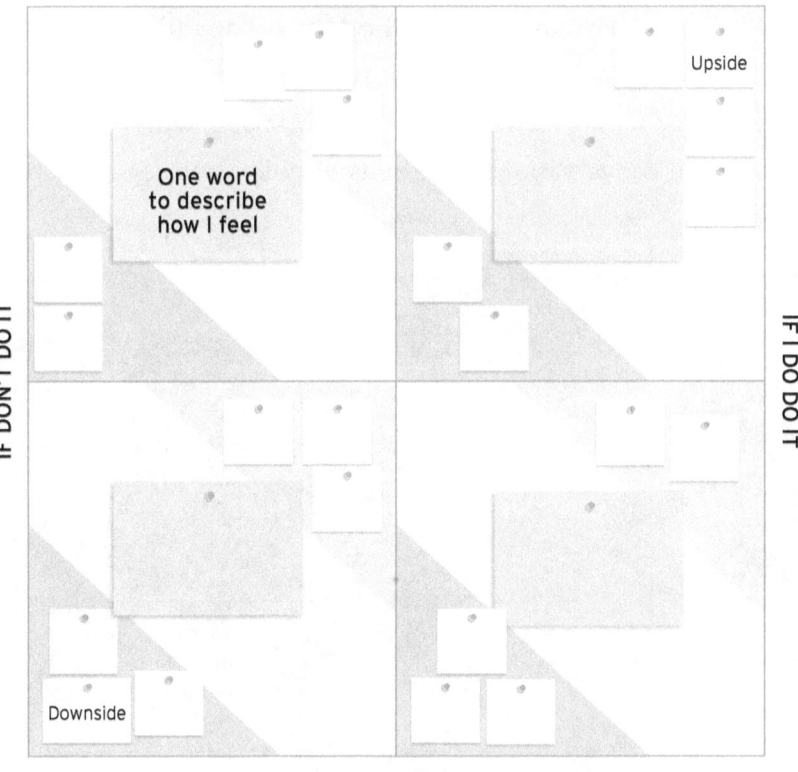

The upsides and downsides of learning motivation

If you are finding it difficult to progress *Project You*, coming up with a label to describe what each of the quadrants feel like as you approach your ONE THING, and what the upsides and downsides might be, can be truly enlightening.

Another way you can think about what's stopping you is by using the voices in your mind that want to 'help' – the same way my cat wants to 'help' me write or work by sitting on the keyboard of my computer. We all have those at some point, don't we (the voices, not cats)? Today, I am calling them Edna (the encourager) and Doris (the doubter). To keep it friendly, I like to think of them as my lovely aunts. Aunt Edna is the quiet one, while Aunt Doris is quite the conversationalist. She is very keen to regularly point

The lovely Aunt Doris and Aunt Edna

out why things won't work, or how I'm not up to doing something because of my many, many character flaws ... you get the idea. But she's family, and I know that she is trying to keep me safe. She doesn't want to see me hurt or disappointed. If you can manage to distract Aunt Doris for a while, you may be able to hear Aunt Edna, who believes in you completely and will quietly, lovingly encourage you to give it a go anyway.

So when you are thinking about the possible upside and downsides of something, particularly if it is your ONE THING, having your aunts' (or you can use celebrities or superheros here) voices in your head could be useful.

Now what?

By doing the exercises to identify what could be stopping you from acting, you will have generated a lot of useful information. So, what to do with it? When you look at your musings on what is getting in the way of your ONE THING, made real by writing them down, you might discover that some reasons resonate with you more than others. Now it's time to work out which ones work for you, which ones don't, and what you are going to do about them.

Know that sometimes awareness is enough. Having your concerns clearly articulated means you are prepared if you find you are putting your foot on the brake unnecessarily. Can you find a different perspective or reframe how you are thinking about things to help unblock you? At other times, what's stopping you may need a little interrogation. If that's the case, talk to someone on *The Team* or do what I like to do and have a chat with your Aunt Doris.

I like to have these conversations out loud and use my hand as a little talking puppet, or sometimes I hand-gesture a phone call. First, I thank Aunt Doris for her concern. Then I add that, after some consideration, I'm still going to be doing my ONE THING and tell her why, and how much it matters to me. And then I ask to speak to Aunt Edna.

As part of this action-packed section we have looked at how to get stuff happening irrespective of our natural tendencies and thought about what might possibly stop us from making things happen. Before that, we grasped the value and importance of reflection and got a few useful tips on how we can implement some reflective practices to support our development. We now also know quite a bit more about how we learn.

Next, we look at getting support and selecting *The Team*. Then later, we'll be putting the whole shebangi together. Keep thinking about your first ONE THING if you haven't decided already, but now it's time to see if we can get a little help around here.

CHAPTER 6
SUPPORT

It is through others that we develop into ourselves.

LEV VYGOTSKY[39]

We now know that self-reflection is important in many contexts and vital for learning. However, when we are reflecting on our actions we can be bad at recognising our own strengths and weaknesses.[40] Social psychologists talk about a common cognitive bias called the 'Dunning-Kruger effect'.[41] This is where the majority of us overestimate our knowledge and abilities in areas of low competence. Studies have shown that when people are asked to rate their abilities, 90 per cent of participants say they are above average – which isn't actually possible.[42]

In other words, because we aren't competent, we don't know

enough to know we aren't competent. It can also mean that in areas where we are highly skilled, we tend to underestimate our abilities because we think everyone knows the stuff we know. This is partly because we are poor at meta-cognition, or the ability to step back and reflect on our abilities from outside ourselves (you remember: our inner Director).[43] As we set about developing our new skills and behaviours, we need to overcome this bias by involving other people. Fortunately for us, this turns out to have a lot of benefits.

We are born totally reliant on others for our survival. For the human species, the support of others is as necessary as food and shelter. In fact, support is so critical to us that the default network in our brain – what we occupy ourselves with when we are not directly focused on a task – uses its time to learn more about our social world. So, when our brain is idling, it's idling in the social world considering what others are doing and unconsciously learning from them.[44]

Somehow, though, the dominant messages in our culture, or the experiences we may have had, separated some of us from valuing connection. Our wont is to be independent, to go it alone, to be a bit of a maverick. Relying on others can be seen as weak. I know I am subject to this in some aspects of my life. I especially love to travel by myself, although, ironically, meeting with unexpected people makes the journey worthwhile. I am constantly amazed at how generous people can be when others need help. I can remember many people – perfect strangers – who offered me kindness, company, food, transport and wine when I was travelling alone. There are people who have helped my career, shared their time and expertise, helped me financially when I was studying, been kind and been forthright. I'm sure you have experienced this human generosity in some way as well. (On the flipside, yes, some people can be arses.)

Such positive experiences can't happen if we don't open ourselves to connecting with others. Learning something new is one of those times when we *should* risk connection rather than go it alone. When learning, we are responsible for our choices, our actions and our inaction. We need the perspectives of others to overcome our biases, and the experience of others to direct us away from some of the pitfalls that may come our way, or to guide us in fruitful – and sometimes unexpected – directions. In the context of *iDevelop*, making connections – or finding *The Team* – will be particularly important in helping you work on your ONE THING as you progress *Project You*.

Who to ask

So let's get some help. But not just from anyone. You need a group of people that will help and support you in various ways, and do so with kindness and honesty. That combination of wonderful people is what we call *The Team*.

Have a think about what you might need from *The Team* – for example, do you need their knowledge? Could you benefit from observing their behaviour? What about the get-along-ability factor? A friend of mine has what she calls her 'Board of Directors' – a group of people she relies on who have different kinds of expertise as well as different roles in her life. Let's make our own now.

What to ask

Here are a few things to consider as you pick out the people who can be on your Board, or *The Team*, for your ONE THING adventure.

1. Are they now, or have they ever been, able to observe you doing or not doing your ONE THING?

Yes, it's probably important to have someone who will from time to time have an opportunity to observe you in your natural habitat (or 'a' natural habitat). It's good to have first-hand observations to draw from. If they are relying on you to report what happened, you may be a little biased or simply not aware of some things. If you are going to invite them onto *The Team* for this project, it is important that they can observe you in action occasionally. If this doesn't occur naturally, you can find a way to make it happen. I frequently ask other facilitators, trainers or speakers to sit in on a session I am conducting. I explain to participants that these people are present to observe me and give me feedback. This is great for my development, but it also normalises the process for others. If this isn't possible, think about someone you worked with in the past, or perhaps someone who knows you outside of work who could potentially observe you in some capacity that would be helpful.

2. Are they someone you can get along with?

You really don't need to be, or possibly want to be, best buds with everyone on *The Team*. But you do need to get along with each *Team* member to a certain extent, and more importantly, understand what they are saying to you. Are they clear communicators, or do you sometimes feel what they talk about is a bit surreal?

Remember, these are people who are not necessarily going to agree with you. They may have different thinking preferences, but it is essential for you to be able to understand them, more or less like them, and feel comfortable enough to ask them anything.

3. Do they have knowledge, experience or expertise relevant to your ONE THING?

Now, this is a one hand/other hand scenario. It could go either way. In some instances, having someone with direct experience will be great. They can act like a mentor, someone who has been there, done that, got themselves the t-shirt and will happily loan it to you. Then there are those people who are great coaches, who will help you to think through what you need to do, even if they don't have direct experience. You will need both at some time, so think about what they are great at and select accordingly.

4. Would they call you out – but kindly – if needed?

When working on your ONE THING, you don't need someone to be your mother and hold your hand, pack your lunch and pick you up late at night – well, not all the time. But you do need someone who will be invested in you succeeding in your efforts. They will be excited when you achieve, kind when you are discouraged and sometimes they will gently hit you with a home truth that leaves you pondering things for a day or so. It will probably hurt. But because it comes from a good place, you know you will get through it – even when it's raw, you'll know this. You really do want this person on your *Team*, and you really want to be the person who wants this kind of help. Keeping it real will get you there.

5. Can you trust them?

Are all the members of your *Team*, or your Board, people you would trust? Learning is a vulnerable state. You may not want *The Team* having discussions at the water cooler, or in a meeting, or with your boss, about things you did or talked about. Setting boundaries is critical. If you have chosen well, you may not need to say to the people on *The Team* to be discreet, but say it anyway.

Seeking advice

There are times when self-reflection gives you a great picture but because you are only looking from your point of view, there can be gaps in your understanding. It's like when you put your finger against a mirror: if it's a regular mirror there will be a little gap between your finger and the reflected image. Despite this gap, remember that even getting this close, even just seeing yourself reflected in the mirror, is way beyond the self-understanding of those who don't ever look.

Two-way glass allows for someone to observe you from another room. You can tell if a mirror has two-way glass because there is no gap. In our context, having someone you know and trust, and who is honest enough to share their perspective with you bridges that gap. With that person helping you, you'll be looking at a two-way mirror: you will see your reflection, but they'll be able to tell you about what they see too. Seeking feedback from someone else can overcome the gaps and biases in your understanding and speed your mastery of your ONE THING.

Identifying two-way glass

MIRROR

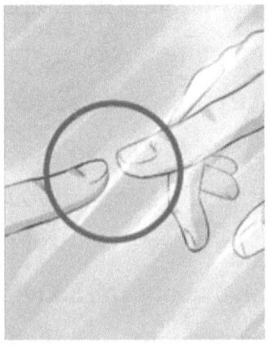

A gap between the reflection and the object means this is a regular mirror.

TWO-WAY GLASS

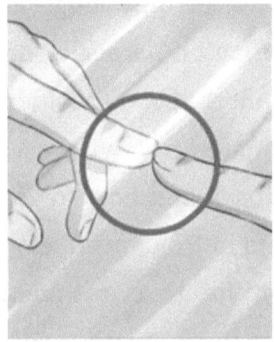

No gaps tells you it is two-way glass and you can be observed

I love to hear someone ask, 'Do I do that?' in a feedback or coaching session. I love it because it provokes self-reflection and questioning. But it can also translate into a new realisation and deeper self-understanding, and be either a very affirming moment, or sometimes a pretty tough one.

I remember providing feedback to a team member – who was going through a period of low confidence at the time – about her great ability to network and how that helps her and others. She hadn't realised that she had this wonderful talent. She even spoke to our team about it, questioning the veracity of my observation. This gave her colleagues an opportunity to share how much she had helped them to navigate several projects, engage with a tricky stakeholder from a different department, and how it made our team more cohesive and effective. It was lovely to watch this realisation dawn on her and watch her confidence grow immediately, as well as seeing the impact of their support flow through our team.

It's not always, or only, hugs and puppies though. There are times when it may be harder to hear what someone is saying to you. It's important that you consider feedback carefully and use the information you are given wisely. We'll take a look at the multiple benefits of feedback and how to go about getting the support you need from others in a balanced way shortly.

In the meantime, here is something to think about: although I talk about 'feedback' in this section, you may want to call it something else. For many, the word 'feedback' can carry a lot of baggage, usually associated with poor or inadequate performance reviews they may have had. At the moment I am also testing out the words 'opinion' and 'advice'. Everyone can get on board with hearing or sharing an opinion. It's just one person's point of view, something to consider. Or feedback can be thought of as a piece advice – like a suggestion. Try subbing in a few different words as you read through this section to see if they feel less threatening for you. You can then try them out in your work environment.

Feedback: it's a gift

Part of *The Team*'s role is to give feedback. And it's true: feedback is a gift. The only drawback is we don't always like the gifts we receive. Ever got a dud present – a moulded-plastic cat fridge magnet; a strangely deformed cardigan? Or the present that really says *I have no idea who you are and what you might like or find useful*: a photo frame? I'm wondering if there is a shop call 'Dud-Gifts-Are-Us' because you would hate to think people worked at getting these things so wrong (ooops … soz). Feedback's a bit like that. It can be just what you always wanted or needed exactly when you need it, or it's a cat fridge magnet.

A fridge magnet no one could love

Like ookie gifts, you may not like or agree with some of the feedback you receive, but you should still be grateful for it. So, when you open the wrapping and find that cat fridge magnet, just say,

'Thank you' and remember that shutting-the-hell-up is an awesome ability.

I know it's hard when people are being critical of something that matters to you. You may feel you need to defend or explain away their perspective. Don't. If you asked for someone's advice or opinion, you simply don't have the right to then say their feedback is wrong. What is being offered to you is one person's perspective of your performance, achievements and behaviour. If it's been given to you and it's not helpful, just say 'thanks' because the next thing might be.

Whether you are actively seeking feedback (and I'll tell you why you should be in a moment), giving feedback or receiving the gift of feedback, approach it with a compassionate heart, a curious mind and a clarity of message in order to make sure your gift arrives in the best possible condition.

Here are a few tips on how you can achieve this.

Be compassionate

Did you know that when we are unkind to someone, we inflict 'social pain'?[45] Ever had a cut on your hand that was very painful? Now, have a look at where it was. Remember how much it hurt and try to feel it. It's hard to recall the experience of physical pain, isn't it? But social pain is the gift that keeps on giving. Recalling that vicious slight from the mean person in Grade 5 sends you straight back to that sunny oval. You can re-experience that pain every time you recall it – that sick feeling in the pit of your stomach, maybe a sense of shame (I'm not bitter). I'm not suggesting it would just be kinder to physically harm someone (although perhaps the research is), but approaching feedback from a place of compassion should be a no-brainer.

Be curious

When seeking, giving or receiving feedback, be curious and test your assumptions. There are many benefits to being curious, despite what those widely reported, and dare I say unsubstantiated, 'killed the cat' rumours say. There is a generosity that exists in being curious that connects us to others. If we are curious to understand what people tell us, we demonstrate that we see and are interested in the other person. If, on the other hand, we want to be right instead, things can spiral downward pretty quickly. Releasing 'your inner Sherlock'[46] in a compassionate manner is good for everyone. As Walt Whitman says, 'Be curious, not judgmental.'

Be clear

In his book *The Advantage*, Patrick Lencioni[47] identifies the four most important things for a healthy organisation. First, he says, build a cohesive leadership team. The other three key aspects this highly regarded business thinker identifies centre on clarity: you need to create *clarity*; over-communicate *clarity*; and reinforce *clarity*. Clarity is such an important thing for how we work and achieve together, and lack of it in an organisation is deadly for its culture.

Before we give, seek or receive feedback we need to be clear about our intention, our message and our needs. Ask yourself if you are seeking, offering or hearing feedback with a compassionate curiosity, or a need based on ego where you want to win or seem smarter than the other person.

All communication is chock-full of potential for misunderstandings. Maybe you feel *you* have expressed something poorly – then be kind, rewind. It might be an underlying tone, an indelicate phrase or just poor timing. Be as certain as you can that the message you are trying to get across is close to the one being heard. (Check out Heidi Grant-Halvorson's book, *No One Understands You and What to do About it* for more on this fascinating topic.)[48]

Plus, know what you want. If you are asking for feedback, make it specific. Not so much, 'So how did I do?' but more, 'Was the way I explained the "curiosity killed the cat" metaphor understandable?' And if you can, let the person giving the feedback know how you prefer your feedback. One of my team members would ask me to give them a general score out of 10 at each catch up – and then would ask what would have made it one point less than that and one point more. Not everyone wants that level of feedback though, so be clear in what you do want.

Feedback: you only need to ask

Heads up if you aren't in the loop on this one. Stop waiting for someone, usually your manager, to give you feedback and start asking (multiple people) for it. In lots of organisations, it's still pretty much expected that our direct manager will provide feedback in our one-on-one meetings or performance appraisal – if you have them. There are two things at work here: the stress of giving and receiving feedback, and the over-reliance on one person only for that feedback – in this case, your manager.

Giving and getting feedback is stressful. The idea and the reality of a manager giving you feedback can put you into what is called an 'away state'.[49] This means thinking about or experiencing performance feedback can switch on your fight, flight or freeze response. In this state, your mind and body feel as though you are under imminent threat – like a tiger is about to pounce and snack on you. Your brain shuts down unnecessary functions except for running away, punching or not moving at all. So, there's not a lot of room for critical thinking, creativity or planning, for example. You can see how that works for a tiger situation, but not so much for a feedback session.

While this may not be the case for you, being reliant on your manager as the only source of feedback can be a bit of an issue if there are 'issues'. This can be especially problematic when linked to a performance appraisal and remuneration. Increasingly, organisations are coming around to the idea that we shouldn't be over-reliant on one person.

Seeking feedback from a range of people and asking specific questions as close to an event as possible is the way to go because it overcomes the two significant concerns discussed. First, it 'de-stresses' the process. The person seeking the feedback is in control and the person whose advice is being sought is usually flattered to be asked.[50] Also, you can decide *who* to ask. Having a range of opinions from a range of people who have observed you in a range of situations is much more productive. Yes, you *could* only ask those who will tell you what you want to hear about yourself, but that would be counterproductive. Plus, if you are reading this book, you are already so much braver than that.

Not all feedback is fun

'Do you think that might have come across as a bit … insensitive?' Whoomph! Ever had a life-changing bit of feedback that hurt like hell, that ran around in your head for the rest of the day, that you tried to explain away but eventually agreed there was something to it? Well, I haven't because I am perfect – obviously – but friends have told me about it happening to them. Sounds tough. Hard to hear, hard to admit to, and courageous on the part of the giver.

In the case of my friend, the person giving the feedback had been compassionate, curious and clear. After some initial queries, she asked me … I mean my 'friend'… if she could share something that needed to be considered but might be a bit hard to hear. She was right, but it was necessary for her to let me … err, my friend … know. And we are probably greater friends because of it … um, I mean, they are …

A final word on *The Team* (for now)

Having run numerous mentoring programs, I know it is common for the mentors to get as much – or more – out of the experience as the mentees. Supporting someone is rewarding and full of learning.

Having said that, it's very important to be clear about what each person can offer in the relationship. Everyone is busy, but if you are both honest about your expectations and realistic about your commitment at the beginning, it will be a much better experience for you both. Remember you have a team, so share the load. That's the point. Not to overburden one person, or rely on one perspective. In chapter 7, we will look at this a little more and talk about how to invite someone onto your team.

Let's summarise what we have learnt so far: hopefully, you are starting to get a grip on the 'who' and the 'how' of support. You'll be thinking about who to select for *The Team* and what you will need from them. Your ONE THING is clear or becoming clearer. You are ready to start balancing reflective and active learning. Great! Because that's what we are going to learn about next.

CHAPTER 7
WHAT ABOUT ME?

*The universe buries strange jewels deep within us all,
and then stands back to see if we can find them.*

ELIZABETH GILBERT[51]

We've done quite a lot of groundwork together so far. You are definitely immersed in the *iDevelop* process. Our next step is to examine the concept of *Project You* in more detail, and discover how to get your first ONE THING happening.

Project You works in three ways: first, through understanding *how* you learn so you can be effective with your ONE THING and anything else you want to learn. Excellent! You've already covered the ways in which people – including you – learn. One down, two to go.

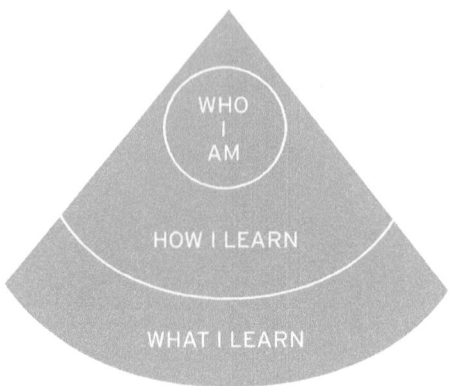

The three aspects of *Project You*

Secondly, it involves identifying *what* the ONE THING you want to learn right now is. No surprises there. Getting that first ONE THING on the way kicks off *Project You* nicely and opens the way for more ONE THINGs in the future.

Lastly, and perhaps most importantly, *Project You* involves making sure your ONE THING builds the knowledge, skills and behaviours that align with who you are and what you value. This is your 'why'. Author James Clear reminds us that 'Every action is a vote for the type of person you want to become.'[52]

You're going to be putting time and effort into your ONE THING, so ideally it should be something that you feel will make your life better, richer and more meaningful in some way. Linking what you value about yourself to what you want to learn is a great motivator for getting the work you need to do done.

Leading business thinker Dan Pink suggests that what motivates people to perform will depend on the type of work they are doing.[53] Extrinsic motivators (rewards, punishment, money) are more likely to suit mechanical or basic skills that do not require a high degree of cognitive input, decision-making or creativity. For work that requires higher order thinking, there are three intrinsic motivators that drive people – autonomy, mastery and purpose. The structure of *Project You* has all three covered: it offers the autonomy to choose how, what and when you develop. Tick. It's the framework that will support you in mastering your series of ONE THINGs. Tick. But then what about your purpose? That is where we are heading now.

Aligning with your purpose

We know that these days it's paramount to keep up to date in our professions but learning ONE new THING well enough to be proficient, or to say that we have mastered it, takes effort and dedication. For most people, that ONE THING can't really be just about the job market. So, what are the other factors that motivate people to pursue learning? And what else could ignite *your* curiosity?

> *The two most important days in your life are the day you are born and the day you find out why.*
>
> **MARK TWAIN**

When identifying the type of learning we most want to do, or our ONE THING, it may be helpful to consider a simple model provided by James Clear (who we met earlier) in his book, *Atomic Habits*.[54] It offers a good understanding of how we can approach any change that impacts our behaviours.

Clear identifies three layers of behavioural change. The first is outcome-focused and is concerned with what you get as a result of your learning, or your goals, such as losing weight or completing a marathon. The next layer is process-focused and it's about what you do, such as swimming every day or not eating carbs. The deepest layer has a focus on identity. This is about what you believe in and focuses on who you can become. In Clears' words: 'It's hard to change your habits if you never change the underlying beliefs that led to your past behaviour. You have a new goal and a new plan, but you haven't changed who you are.'[55]

That's what we mean when talking about getting clear on your purpose. We continue to develop ourselves in order to become

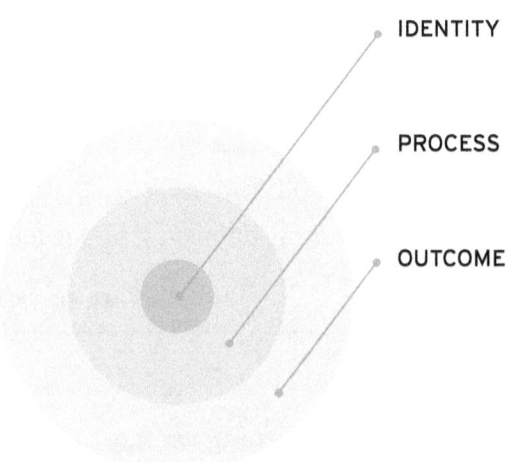

Levels of behavioural change

more aligned with what matters most to us. You may have heard it described as 'becoming more of who we are'.

One way of doing this is discussed by leadership specialists Nick Craig and Scott Snook. They suggest creating a clear statement about your purpose keeping the following in mind:

> *Purpose is definitely not some jargon-filled catch-all ('Empower my team to achieve exceptional business results while delighting our customers'). It should be specific and personal, resonating with you and you alone. It doesn't have to be aspirational or cause-based ('Save the whales' or 'Feed the hungry'). And it's not what you think it should be. It's who you can't help being. In fact, it might not necessarily be all that flattering ('Be the thorn in people's side that keeps them moving!').*[56]

Remember, understanding your purpose and being able to explain why it motivates you is hugely beneficial in itself. It can also shift our understanding of what we are currently doing or not doing and lead us to prioritise what actions might be important for us to focus on.

Clarifying your purpose

If you are having trouble deciding on your ONE THING, or what it is you want to achieve by working on *Project You*, some creative thinking can get your mind in the right space. Here are a few exercises that might help you work towards some clarity.

QUESTIONS TO CONSIDER

» Ask yourself some questions that draw on your past. Craig and Snook suggest that the following three can be quite effective. Try reflecting on:
- an activity you loved doing as a child before the world told you what to like and do; focus on how one specific shiny moment made you feel
- how one or two of your most challenging life experiences shaped you
- something you enjoy doing in your life right now that helps you sing your song.

» Draw a line across the middle of a big sheet of paper representing your life up to now. Mark in some stages – your first memory, you at five years old, then at primary school, then as a teenager, etc. Above the line, indicate incidents that made you happy; below the line, note things that were not so great. Can you identify any consistent themes?

» Imagine your life as a movie, book or magazine. Come up with a title and draw the cover or poster.

These points won't take you directly to a clear statement of intent but will prompt your thinking and provide a little clarity on what direction you might take. Doing this takes a little time and reflection, so it's probably best done over a couple of sessions. What you are looking to create is a short, punchy statement about what you would like to do. It should be personal or meaningful just to you, not bland corporate-speak, because this isn't anything you need to share.

Craig and Snook offer this example of what not to have as your statement of intent: '[I must] continually and consistently develop and facilitate the growth of myself and others leading to great performance.' Yep, very jargon-y. Here is what they suggest it could be: 'With tenacity, create brilliance.' Can you create a statement that resonates with you?

Choose your own adventure

Some people know exactly what they want to learn to move them to the next thing. If that's you, great. Let's go! It wouldn't hurt for you to read this section though. It will give you some insight on those not blessed with your powers of decision-making. (You know who they are because you often find working or going to dinner with them very frustrating.)

> 'Would you tell me, please, which way
>   I ought to go from here?'
> 'That depends a good deal on where you
>   want to get to,' said the Cat.
> 'I don't much care where –' said Alice.
> 'Then it doesn't matter which way you go.'
>
> LEWIS CARROLL, *ALICE IN WONDERLAND*

Those who are uncertain about what to focus on for their learning – their first ONE THING – might be struggling with a few questions such as: What do I do first? What's the most important thing to do now? How ambitious should I be with my goal? How will I ever choose? The fear of making the wrong decision can paralyse people into indecision. If this is you, let me share an important piece of information about your first ONE THING with you: it doesn't matter what you choose, just choose *something*.

I'm not saying it's not important, just that making this decision is your first huge milestone, and by making it, you will be ready to move on. Learning something new is rarely a bad thing, and even if it's the fifth most important ONE THING you could learn, that's fine – you can get to the others later. When you do choose your next ONE THING, you'll be better at deciding because you have done it once already. Plus, you'll then be one of those people who can just decide.

Having said that, don't just open the dictionary and put a pin in something – well not yet. Let's check something first. Sometimes, people (not you, though) will be inclined to say they don't know what they want to do but haven't really done anything about it. It's not a lack of decision-making that is the problem, just a lack of effort. You need to put a little effort into thinking about your ONE THING. Now, I know this won't be you, but say your ONE THING hasn't just popped into your head. How much thinking have you done about this? And for how long? How much effort have you really put into it? Be honest with yourself. If you haven't done the pondering required as yet, here are three things you can use to resource your thinking – self-reflection, asking others and looking at some data.

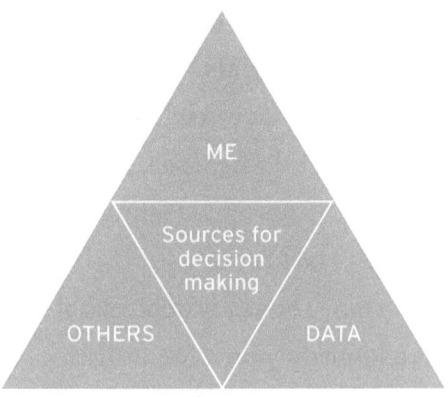

Sources for decision making

Reflect

In chapter 3, we took a good look at how to develop a reflective practice. However, let's acknowledge that for some people self-reflection will be a little uncomfortable. It might seem a bigger and more difficult thing to do than they think.

Reflection on what we do and want to do is important and can be complex, but what I'm talking about here is you taking a little time to think about what you know about you (surprisingly, not everyone's best subject) and asking a few questions. It doesn't have to be complicated. Here are a couple of things to consider before you plunge in:

Think about your environment. You will need a little clear space to give yourself some room to think. Can you set up some alone time? Do you focus best in a quiet green nature-y spot, by the lapping of water, in the library, while jogging or in a bustling coffee shop? Do you have what you need – phone (to record audio notes), notebook, computer, pens, drawing materials?

Check your mindset. Maybe you feel like really getting stuck into this work. Maybe you don't. Either way, you need to get your head around doing the work. If you are feeling resistant, what is that about? Perhaps you can start there.

Okay, got those sorted? Let's now apply what we learnt in chapter 3 about reflection to identify your ONE THING.

Below is a list of questions to ask yourself that can help prompt your thinking. You can write your answers down, but I suggest you look at the list of activities that accompany the list of questions too. These are creative ways to get ideas flowing. I recommend you do something a little out of the box – choose an activity that you don't necessarily feel comfortable with, something that stretches you a little. Even if the result doesn't turn out like you hoped, it will still be a useful exercise – and maybe even fun.

QUESTIONS TO REFLECT ON

Note: Some of these will resonate more than others, so choose one or two and go wild.

What do I need to develop to be a 'me' I'd like to get to know better?	It's a little obvious, but sometimes we don't make the time and space for thinking about who we are and where we are going. Who do you want to be? What do you want to be known for?
What's the most important thing I can do with my time?	We are not here for a long time, so we may as well make it count. What would that mean for you?
What do I forget to stop doing?	'Flow' is what happens when you get so immersed in an activity that you lose yourself. You are not aware of time passing, or distractions. You perform effortlessly and are deeply content.[57] What are the types of activities where this happens to you?
What will people say about me when I retire?	Imagine you are about to retire. You're at a party, but one that you like because your colleagues, peers and family are celebrating you and the career you had. What are they saying? What did you do in your working life? Focus on a best-ever version of this where you acted to develop and grow the work-life you want. Then focus on a worst-case scenario where you did nothing and think about what that would look like. Try on several versions for size and see which you would like to aim for and which you'd like to avoid.
Who do I envy?	Is there someone you look at and think, **Wow! I really wish I was more like that person?** We are talking a behaviour or a skill rather than some physical characteristic. Maybe they are cool under pressure or seem to be commercially savvy, or great with people.
What else?	There's lots more to think about here – let your mind go free. I'm sure you can think of other questions too!

ACTIVITIES TO HELP YOU FOCUS AND REFLECT

Note: You need to do more than simply think about these questions. Get creative. Make it fun. Allow ideas to surface and see where you get. Don't judge your ability - you are just getting ideas. Above all, enjoy the process.

Find an object	Is there an object in your environment that you can look to for inspiration? Sometimes just the act of focusing on an object, like a leaf, painting or street sign can get us thinking. Humans love making meaning, so consider what your object may represent about what you need.
Draw a picture	Choose your medium (watercolour, colouring pencils, pastels, acrylic paints). Get lots of paper, or a cheap canvas if you like, then draw anything that was prompted by your questions.
Create a mind map	If you are not a keen drawer - which is a great reason to do the drawing activity anyway - try brainstorming with yourself to make a network of your ideas. Write down key words that could work as a trigger for you and note where you think they might lead.
Write a story	You could either journal your thoughts or try answering one of the questions by telling a fairytale, romance, sci-fi or thriller. Come up with a book title and then use that as inspiration. Create a story. Go old school and write it in a nice notebook or go digital and design it on a tablet or laptop.
Make a Play-Doh model	This tactile activity is not to be underestimated. You can buy Play-Doh or make it cheaply. The act of answering a question using colourful mushy stuff can be quite profound.

Don't sweat it if these exercises and your reflection time don't get you to your ONE THING just yet. The next tip you can try is asking around. Lucky you've done all that reflecting. By thinking about things, you'll have plenty of information to consider and share with others.

Ask around

You've done some reflecting, given the Play-Doh a go. It might be useful at this point to check in with some other people to get a couple of outside perspectives on your ONE THING and how you could develop while doing your *Project You*. If I haven't said this already (and that's not very likely, really), learning is a team game. Getting fresh perspectives from others, as well as a bit of support, can help you get clear on what you'd like to do.

I am pretty sure you know some people who would be only too happy to offer their opinions about how you could develop into being a better version of you. But that's where *The Team* comes in. In chapter 6, we looked at gathering *The Team*, how to select the right people and how they can help. This is a great place to start using their perspectives. Asking for their opinion or advice now will really engage them in your journey.

Having said that, asking others for help doesn't always come naturally. Talking about something that makes you a little vulnerable, and is important to you, can be tricky. Does the thought of this conversation fill you with dread? Or is it something you can't wait to have? Or do you already do this regularly or easily?

Regardless of how you feel about it, you do need to remember that when you ask for someone's perspective, that's what you'll get: a perspective. Not a fact. It's an opinion – their opinion. They are allowed to have one. You are allowed to ask to hear it.

What happens next is up to you. Take it on board, ignore it, whatever. Just remember to listen. You can ask for examples or to have something clarified, but don't argue, rationalise or explain. Most importantly – and you'll remember this from chapter 6 – say, 'Thank you'. Not, 'Thank you, I see where you are coming from with the bit about ...', but simply, 'Thank you.' If you really can't stop yourself at two words, try, 'Thank you, I appreciate that.' Ultimately, you are the one who will decide what you want to do with the information.

Also, if you get a suggestion from someone you respect and trust that blindsides you, don't panic. This could be a positive comment you weren't expecting – lovely, not a problem. Something you could live up to more fully. However, it may be a comment that hurts or stings a little. Try not to become reactive. Take a breath. Ask for other people's perspectives, but not in a 'Do you know what Bill/Mary said about me ...' way. Just be curious. Remember, your brain is going to want to hang on to it and blow it out of proportion for you (not helpful).

If others also have this perception, brace yourself. It might be useful to recall the seven stages of grief – shock, denial, anger, bargaining, depression, testing and acceptance. It might also be useful to recall that this is a perception – it might be right, it might be wrong, it might even be useful, but it can definitely be changed.

And remember you have allies –yes, *The Team*! – to support and help you work things out.

Now that you know who to talk to and are more prepared for feedback, let's take a brief look at how you might start this conversation:

ONE THING

- » You: Hey [insert trusted advisor's name here]! How are you?
- » [Insert required amount of personable chitchat here]
- » If you've got a few minutes, I'd like to talk to you about something. I'm thinking of doing some professional development, but I really want to focus on ONE THING that could make a difference to [insert your purpose, e.g. improve my customer service, how I support my team]. You have [worked with me/seen me working with others/another scenario].
- » Is there ONE THING you think would be a good area for me to focus on right now?

Get data

Another way to find some clarity around your ONE THING is to think about any potential data that may help. Hmm … data? If you already have access to some performance data, or a profiling tool to help clarify or solidify your choice, then that's great. However, not every organisation will have these so I've put together some potential sources of useful data that could help you choose your ONE THING.

Performance management

Performance management is undergoing a rethink in many organisations so this type of experience can be quite varied. In the last five or so years, the focus has shifted from a rigid annual assessment scored against key performance indicators that are rated, ranked and linked to remuneration, to a focus on the importance of regular conversations held between a manager and their employee. These days, employees are also likely to be encouraged to seek feedback from a broad range of sources on a specific area for development and to do so in a timely manner – that is, close to the actual event being reviewed.

Performance management can often be a combination of these approaches. It can be used to look at a team or an individual. Sometimes they are done well and are effective and at other times, less so.

Whatever way these are conducted at your workplace, this is a great place to start. The good thing is that most systems include your perspective along with the reviewer's. Usually there is a combination of qualitative and quantitative information. Some aspects are scored against a category, such as goals and capabilities. Even if the data is not quantified, there can be some rich qualitative data in comments and summaries.

There is also usually a strong focus on areas for development. It can be interesting and useful to go back over your thoughts and those of your manager or other reviewers. It gives you the opportunity to question which areas you followed up, which may need greater focus, and anything that may have fallen by the wayside because of other priorities.

360° feedback

Another widely used tool that can provide information to help identify that ONE THING you want to learn is 360° feedback. For the uninitiated, this involves the participant selecting several people they work with and inviting them to complete a questionnaire. The respondents include managers, peers, employees who report to the participant, other stakeholders and the participant themselves. The selection of people who are above, below and beside them in their organisational hierarchy gives the participant a 360° perspective of their performance – hence the name.

The questionnaire can focus on things such as leadership, emotional intelligence or general performance. You and the respondents score your performance on specific areas of capability. When done well, 360° feedback can offer some great insights into how you believe you are performing and how others perceive your performance. Others can often see our areas of strength and where we are challenged more clearly than we can. Getting a range of perspectives could help you choose just the ONE THING you need.

Psychometric assessments and profiling instruments

There are many popular profiling tools that can assist you in identifying your ONE THING. Some organisations will provide these as part of their learning program. These types of tools use a series of questions to measure things like ways of thinking, motivation, values, abilities, attitudes, personality traits and work preferences. With a few exceptions, they are non-judgmental, which means there are no right or wrong answers.

It is not essential for you to do one of these, but they can help with self-awareness and may bring to light why you think or act in a particular way – and why others can be so very different from you. Listed below are a few of the more popular tools you could try.

TOOL	WHAT IS IT AND HOW IS IT USED?
Core Values Index (CVI™)	CVI™ helps people focus on identifying what satisfies or fulfils them about the work they do. It matches motivational drivers with the core responsibilities of a role by measuring innate preference (suitability) rather than ability or adaptability.
DiSC®	DiSC® takes its name from the four primary behavioural traits it measures: Dominance (D), Influence (I), Steadiness (S) and Conscientiousness (C), and provides an understanding of the way people think, act and interact.
Gallop's CliftonStrengths Finder	CliftonStrengths assessments identify your unique talents so you can do more of what you are great at every day. It uncovers your strengths in building relationships, thinking strategically, influencing others and accomplishing goals.
Herrmann Brain Dominance Instrument® (HBDI®)	HBDI® measures and describes thinking preferences in people under normal and stressed situations, in order to help them learn how to communicate effectively, improve decision-making and enhance problem solving.
Hogan Assessments	Hogan offers a range of assessments to help identify people's strengths (the bright side), challenges (the dark side) and values (the inside), and also help in predicting performance.

Life Styles Inventory™ (LSI™) by Human Synergistics	The LSI™ assesses thinking styles, personal effectiveness, and satisfaction at work and home. It identifies individual thinking and behavioural styles and provides insights into strengths and areas for development.
Myers-Briggs Type Indicator (MBTI®)	The MBTI® is a widely used tool designed to indicate psychological preferences. It provides insights into how people perceive the world and make decisions in order to improve individual, team and organisational performance.
Occupational Personality Questionnaire (OPQ)	The OPQ is a trait-based measure of an individual's personality preferences in the workplace. It focuses on relationships with people, thinking style, and feelings and emotions.
Team Management Profile (TMP)	The TMP is a psychometric profiling tool that identifies a person's strengths and work preferences, and is used for personal, team and leadership development.
VIA Character Strengths	The VIA Character Strengths survey measures an individual's character strengths. These are our positive personality or core capacities for thinking, feeling and behaving in ways that can bring benefit to us and to others.

Strengths or weaknesses?

It's likely that the majority of the data you'll gather will offer you at least some insight into yourself and into what that ONE THING you need to learn right now might be. But there are still some questions to ask yourself when assessing your data: What should you focus on? Should you identify your strengths and leverage your existing abilities? Or should you identify any 'skills gaps' or 'opportunities for development' (because calling them a weakness is largely frowned upon)?

> *Play a game that favors your strengths.*
> *If you can't find a game that favors you, create one.*
>
> JAMES CLEAR[58]

This can be a tricky choice to make. The idea of 'working with your strengths' is based on the understanding that our talents are unique and enduring, so it is said that developing our strengths is our greatest opportunity for growth.[59] But some researchers are concerned that focusing only on our strengths may be detrimental,[60] and suggest that although it is good to do so, it's a poor strategy in the long run if you have a serious weakness.[61] Hmm ... helpful.

Whichever way you go, it's important to keep in mind when choosing your ONE THING to select what will work best for you right now. You could expand or deepen your knowledge of something you are already strong in, or choose to develop and improve something you are not terribly good at. Remember also that if you choose to go with your strengths this time for your ONE THING, you could choose to improve on a weakness for your next ONE THING as you continue on your *Project You* journey. You'll be learning either way, so it's a win/win situation.

Still deciding?

I can't tell you how important deciding is ... but I am going to try. One thing a mentor still tells me repeatedly is that the first sale is to yourself. If you don't believe that what you are selling will add value to someone's life, then no one else will either. So, in this context, if you don't believe what you are going to do will make a difference to *your* life, you are putting yourself at a huge disadvantage before you even get started. You can easily set yourself up to fail, which is not ideal as we all need some things to go well to stay motivated.

Still feel like you have a million things you could do and are paralysed by the choice? You've reflected, asked around and reviewed the data ... hopefully you've narrowed it down to a final few choices ... but you still can't decide on your ONE THING? It's time to consider three final things that could influence your choice – passion, sequence and availability.

Passion

Feeling passionate about what you will be working on for *Project You* is important for your success. Your passion will help you but won't take you the whole way. But if you really can't decide, go with your gut. What do you have a good feeling about?

> *Let yourself be silently drawn by the strange*
> *pull of what you really love.*
>
> RUMI

Sequence

Sometimes there is a natural order for learning. What would naturally come first? Is there a ONE THING that you might need to do before you can do that other ONE THING? Try writing your choices on sticky-notes and ranking them. Once again, ask someone who knows you well. What would they think would be the best first ONE THING to do? Looking at the order of things here will help you eliminate some options and highlight those that could build a good foundation for further development.

Availability

Maybe there is ONE THING you really want to do, but the best learning opportunity is not immediately available. There is a course you want to do that doesn't start for a month or so. An expert in the field you are interested in will be presenting soon at a conference. A favourite or respected author is releasing the exact book you'll need to work on your ONE THING. If there is a very good reason to delay choosing or starting your ONE THING it could be better to wait – but make sure you don't use any of these as an excuse not to decide or start at all.

Now decide already!

Finally, just pick that ONE THING, knowing there will be more ONE THINGs later. All the other ONE THINGs are not leaving the planet, so don't worry. If you really can't identify the perfect thing to learn, don't let needing to nut this out be a barrier to learning. We can often get hung up on doing the perfect thing when we would benefit enormously from simply doing something. Don't aim for perfect, aim for perfect-ish.[62] Gaining any new knowledge or learning, any new skills and behaviours, will benefit you and potentially allow you to help others.

Whatever you decide, don't forget that you must take responsibility for your choice and be ready to give it a red-hot go. Peter Bregman, an authority on leading organisations, describes an experience when his son was feeling despondent about succeeding at soccer. He first asked his son, 'Do you want to get better [at soccer]?' The boy answered, 'Yeah.' Bregman then asked a second question: 'Are you willing to feel the discomfort of putting in more effort and trying new things that will feel weird and different and won't work right away?'[63]

Doing the work is essential for self-development of any kind. But as the quote suggests, it's important to acknowledge that even if you are willing to put in the work, and willing to perhaps choose a ONE THING that is perfect-ish so that you can get started, you may still have moments of doubt.

You will most likely question your decision somewhere along the line: 'This isn't the ONE THING I should be doing!'; 'There are more urgent things to do'; 'I'm not really passionate enough about this ONE THING to stick at it'; 'It's hard.' All really good reasons for doubt, but not good enough reasons for giving up.

So, why make the commitment to your ONE THING? Why make the effort to do the work and see it through?

Do it for no other reason than opening yourself to the surprising little gifts that this whole ONE THING experience will give you. Unexpected, possibly wonderful, things will happen, especially if you seek them out.

CHAPTER 8
FINDING INFORMATION

Know where to find the information and how to use it — that's the secret of success.

ALBERT EINSTEIN

In chapter 2, we discussed the 70:20:10 learning model that states we learn predominantly through experience or by actively doing things (70 per cent); partly through the exposure to networks, mentors and coaches (20 per cent); and also through education or more formal learning (10 per cent). While it is the smallest part of the equation, formal education is still important. This is the part that looks at what the experts in the field, who impart their wisdom through formal education programs, workshops, journals and books, have to say about your topic. This is where we get ideas and learn new information; reflect on these ideas in relation to our context; think about how we can incorporate this into our practice; and then see if it all works. Hmm, now that was probably just a long way to say, 'Learn about a great idea and try it out'!

When we are learning from others (20) or by doing (70), we want to be learning efficiently, effectively and ethically. We don't want to learn to do things in the hardest way possible, or learn that thing in a way that doesn't work, or in a way that can get us (or anyone else) hurt or imprisoned. Therefore, knowing how to find good content is important when you are starting out on a new way of doing something. It helps to compare and explore what your networks and mentors are telling you with what other experts say, so you can broaden your understanding and even challenge their perceived wisdom – because everyone has new things to learn and share.

This doesn't only apply to when you are learning something new. 'Education' (10) as we are talking about it here also applies to how we continue to nurture and refine something we are currently doing, so that *we* can become the experts and can go on to coach and mentor others. Education is not just a workshop or a degree, it includes the many resources out there that are created by experts who are not available to mentor you or work with you personally.

Content is everywhere. Information on the ONE THING you want to learn is out there in abundance. It has never been easier to find useful information – and along with it, lots of really useless stuff too.

In a lovely analogy, organisational psychologist Tomas Chamorro-Premuzic suggests that in the past, we had too little food and low environmental stimulation. Today (although not equally or everywhere), we live in a world full of low-nutrient, high-calorie food and are exposed to a highly stimulating environment. The over-stimulation of our (particularly digital) environment, like the impact of plentiful yet poor-quality food on our diet, is proving harmful to our health and society. He says that with so much information available, 'it is now more advantageous to ignore new information than to absorb it'.[64]

Well, in order to learn our ONE THING, we don't want to ignore *all* of that information. We need to get the good stuff! We need to know how to sort out the useful from the useless. How do we go about finding reliable sources that will be valuable to us? Where do we look? How do we know what's good, and who can help us if we are stuck?

This chapter is designed to answer these questions and provide you with guidance on finding the right information for you and your ONE THING. Here we go.

Look Here

Having decided what you want to develop (with the help of the previous chapter, of course!), let's think about where some great resources may reside. This section is about moving beyond reflective practice and gaining new information to help you learn, or unlearn then relearn differently, your ONE THING. Looking at our model, you'll see this kind of work located in the top left quadrant, under what is identified as 'independent learning'.

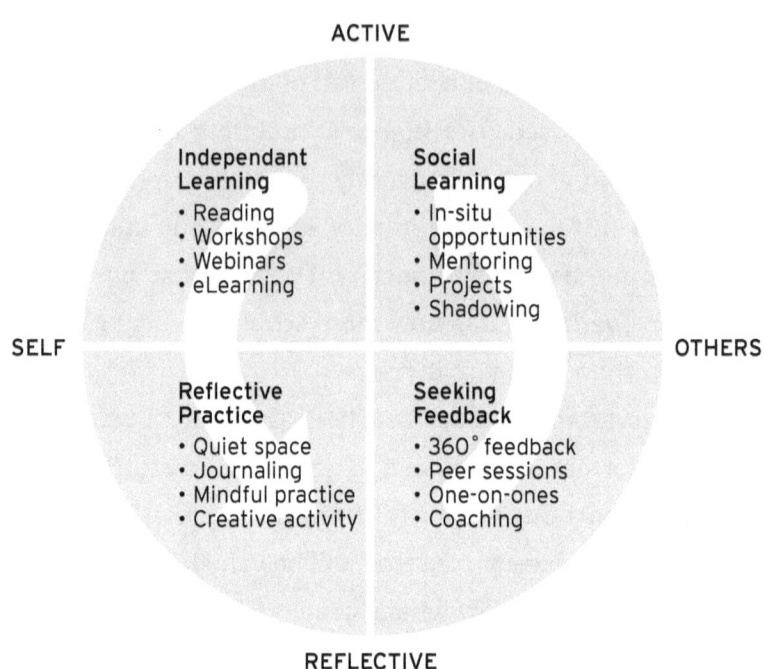

Examples for the iDevelop Learning Model

If we think about the potential sources we could use, we can break them into what I'll call 'digital' and 'physical'. It's not a perfect delineation, but it's a good start. Digital sources refer to anything you can get online, and physical is anything that you can't. These contain four main modes – 'read', 'watch', 'listen' and 'do'. People tend to have preferred modes, and each one comes with its upsides and downsides.

Sourcing great content

The following table is designed to show you at a glance the many options we now have when looking for information.

	PHYSICAL	DIGITAL
READ	Books Magazines Academic journals Newspapers	eBooks eMagazines Online journals Digital newspapers Condensed books Blogs Social/business platforms
WATCH	Theatre and art events	Vlogs Videos Online TED Talks
LISTEN	Lectures and speeches	Audio books Podcasts Radio
DO	Workshops	Webinars MOOCS eLearning

Mode 1: Read

This mode is all about that miraculous little system of symbols we've invented for communication. You are reading them now, and they have created some magical and revolutionary changes to our world – yes, that's letters, words and writing. Reading is something we can do across many mediums, physical or digital. I am just a little bit in love with reading – that's because there is a myriad of publications, both online and on paper, that have the ability to spark our imaginations and are out there just waiting to help you as you learn and develop your ONE THING.

Physical reading

Reading in general tends to be handy, inexpensive and portable – it's anytime, anywhere learning. Plus, there are these people called 'librarians' who you can talk to at your local library. In major state and university libraries, you may be able to find librarians who are experts in specific fields, say business or engineering. They are very helpful and lovely people.

For those who love reading, there's good news: books, magazines, journals and newspaper are not going anywhere, although some of them are changing form. There has been a lot made of the demise of physical publications – actual things printed on paper – but it's not all doom and gloom if that is your information source of choice. Books are still popular, with sales reported as being on the rise, even outselling eBooks in some cases.[65]

Here are some ideas of where to find things to read and what to keep in mind.

UPSIDES	DOWNSIDES	THINGS TO CONSIDER
BOOKS		
Relatively inexpensive Readily available Cover every topic you need to know and lots you'll never need to know ... ever	They get wet in the bath (well, everything does, but the point is it makes them harder to read)	If you are new to a topic, consider reading the classic text, the contemporary classic and the latest to get a good flavour of the field Someone at a good bookstore or library can help you find what you need, or you can ask a knowledgeable peer to recommend titles
MAGAZINES		
As above There are some very good quality magazines available for getting to grips with workplace matters, e.g. *Harvard Business Review; Forbes; Inc.; Fast Company; WIRED* (for emerging technologies) Articles can give you a flavour of a topic quickly	Think about the source - is *New Women's Day Weekly Idea* magazine necessarily going to be helpful?	Useful to spark further research if you want to go deep, or a place to identify smaller ONE THINGs to try in between (or concurrent with) big ONE THINGs

JOURNALS		
Academic journals are peer-reviewed - important for quality research Usually offer detailed, rigorous analysis	Some aspects of peer-review are under question Can be difficult to access some publications	Some can be a technical and/or dense read, especially across a whole field of study, so care needs to be taken not to overinterpret or misinterpret the information presented.
NEWSPAPERS		
Topical - can give you a flavour of current or popular thinking on a topic Good for book reviews and some articles Can be useful for generating ideas across topics	Bit unpredictable - hard to know what you'll find of value on a daily basis	Good for staying informed about what's happening in general

Digital Reading

The popularity of digital reading is still reasonably new – the Kindle was launched in 2007 – but it's increasing. Nearly anything you can find bound in paper can be found online too, and much more. Short, long, academic, popular, expert, novice, research, opinion – it's all there. Here we look at a number of sources you can consider in your search for ONE THING information.

UPSIDES	DOWNSIDES	THINGS TO CONSIDER
EBOOKS, EMAGAZINES, ONLINE JOURNALS, DIGITAL NEWSPAPERS		
What applies to physical reading generally applies here More easily searchable Even if your source is subscription-based, often a few articles will be free Google Scholar can help you with peer-reviewed journals.[66]	Some subscriptions can be costly	eBooks usually have a note-taking and highlighting function that make it easier to retrieve the things you find important and interesting
CONDENSED BOOKS[67]		
Let's you get your head around key themes As they are generally short, you can increase the volume and diversity of what you read	There is a cost to subscribe You can't get certain nuances of the complete book Not every book will be available, but there is lots of choice	You can use it as an environmental scan of what's out there It's great for getting an idea of which books you may want to go into more deeply
SOCIAL PLATFORMS		
Good for getting a feel for the latest things	The latest thing might not be the best (novelty ≠ excellence) Watch for confirmation bias if your feed is from friends and people who think like you	Sorry, too busy watching that cat video … again.

Mode 2: Watch

When discussing watchable sources with content that may be useful for our ONE THING, we mostly think about moving images (is there another word for this unrelated to the format? Video, film, DVD?). The combination of visual and audio is irresistible to many of us. It holds our interest through colour and movement, and captures our emotions with music and sound. It is hypnotic. Everyone is creating video content these days and many people now prefer this mode of discovering information over other, more traditional methods.

Confession ahead, though – I really had to think a bit tangentially to come up with something physical for this, but there are options out there that can offer you a different way of getting inspiration.

Physical watching

This type of watching relates to information created to support learning rather than pure observation of nature or people or events. Maybe this is not something that you would think of immediately (I know I didn't), but going to live art events could certainly be one way of gaining inspiration. A gallery exhibition or theatre performance, for example, could spark the very ONE THING you are looking for.

UPSIDES	DOWNSIDES	THINGS TO CONSIDER
THEATRE, ARTS		
It's novel and, although you may not specifically learn about your ONE THING, novelty makes information more sticky It's fun!	It may not only be about your ONE THING Can be costly, but not always	There may be a more direct route to the information (however, if this is something you enjoy, stay alert to possibility!)

Digital watching

Video content is the bomb these days, but you need to consider what is going to be valuable for you and your ONE THING. Vlogs (video blogs) are very popular. This is where people video their thoughts, opinions, or experiences and publish them on the internet. There are also other sources for information sharing in this medium, often found on video-sharing platforms like YouTube and Vimeo, where anyone can post content. For getting content relevant to your ONE THING, a TED Talk could also be a good place to start.

UPSIDES	DOWNSIDES	THINGS TO CONSIDER
VLOGS		
Wide range of content Usually a record of a personal experience	Personal experience and observations can be well considered and useful but not always.	You'll need to check the accuracy of the information by seeking out multiple sources and looking for counter arguments

VIDEO (YOUTUBE, VIMEO, ETC.)		
Wide range of content Can be a record of a personal experience, created by a business, or purely educational Often highly engaging	If it has cats in it, you are in distraction mode - stop immediately	It's best to think about why this content has been produced and whether or not it is really applicable to your ONE THING
TED TALKS		
Short speeches on a diverse range of topics Delivered by subject-matter experts	You can overdose and get sucked into the mire that is TED-Talk addiction	These can be quite motivating if you are feeling a little low - try popping one on at lunchtime or during a break when you need a lift

Mode 3: Listen

This is about content that you hear – obviously. Some people find learning this way very engaging and effective. Hearing a person who is a specialist in a field you are interested in, or someone with a lot of experience associated with your ONE THING, can inspire and encourage your learning. If this is your preferred mode, the following are some avenues for you to explore.

Physical listening

Attending a lecture or speech in person is a great way to find content. If you are doing a university or TAFE course, these will most likely be part of the curriculum. Even if you are not enrolled in a formal degree or qualification and find a course that may have some helpful content, you could contact the lecturer and ask them if you could sit in on a class. There are also many opportunities out there for the general public to hear experts speak at public forums or conferences.

UPSIDES	DOWNSIDES	THINGS TO CONSIDER
LECTURES AND SPEECHES		
The experience of being in the presence of a talented orator with a great message is not to be missed Can offer you an opportunity to ask questions	You might not catch all the content, or be able to record them	It can be hard to find – check sites like Eventbrite, live TED Talks in your areas, or take a look at specific speaker's website for dates and venues

Digital listening

I am a bit funny with digital listening. I'm a huge fan of the radio – especially ABC Radio National. I will often turn it on in the early hours of the morning if I am unable to sleep. I find I learn wondrous, unexpected things. I am late to the podcast phenomena but getting to like it. However, and this is just me, I am not a fan of audiobooks. I am happy to listen to them when I am on the move or doing another task, but I can't write things down easily, or see the diagrams, or take the quiz while listening. They don't feel like they are enough for me. I used them for a while, but found I needed to purchase the digital or print version as well. But I know other people who love, love, love them.

UPSIDES	DOWNSIDES	THINGS TO CONSIDER
AUDIO BOOKS		
Not very costly A great range Highly portable	Visual learners can't see the words, images or models	Great for doing in conjunction with dissimilar activities
PODCASTS		
Mostly free A vast range Available on demand	Sources need to be checked for quality of information and potential for bias	Can be addictive!
RADIO		
It's free Available on demand You can sometimes download transcripts	Sources need to be checked for quality of information and potential for bias	This is such an under-utilised resource – ABC Radio National's archives are well worth checking out because they're good and they belong to us

Mode 4: Do

Keep in mind that this section is about finding content for your ONE THING – not about applying what you have learnt. That's the part that will be up to you later. But being more actively engaged in learning from the beginning can help you embed the information you are trying to learn more deeply into your mind. Whether this is physically attending a face-to-face workshop or facilitated session, or engaging in interactive online programs, your participation helps shape the session for yourself and others.

Physical doing

Workshops focus on developing a single skill (or several) and rely on your participation in order for you to learn. It's a two-way thing where you get to interact, practice things, and hear different opinions and approaches from the group and the trainer. It's not simply a lecture. Larger organisations may have their own teams for delivering their own content. They may also buy in professional expertise or send employees to public courses.

Running something in-house that is delivered exclusively to employees of the organisation can enable consistent messaging and communication of knowledge, as well as build connections across, or within, specific teams or groups. This can be very useful, particularly if your ONE THING can benefit from this type of content.

In contrast, attending a publicly run course enables you to mix with people from other organisations and can give you new perspectives and solutions to take back to your workplace. Keep that in mind as you are selecting a workshop or training program and decide where you would gain the most value in developing your ONE THING.

UPSIDES	DOWNSIDES	THINGS TO CONSIDER
WORKSHOPS		
Can be very instructive and conducted in a fun and interactive way You meet and learn from other people with different perceptions, perspectives and experiences	They are rarely free and sometimes quite costly The content may not be at the right level - there may be stuff you already know, or that is beyond your current skill level Other people might be distracting or unhelpful There may not be a lot of opportunity to interact or practise	Is the content on-topic for your ONE THING? Is it at the level you require? Is there enough time allowed for the content to be delivered adequately? Is there any follow-up support available? Can you get recommendations from other participants, or enquire about their experiences?

Digital doing

Getting content online that is interactive in some way is popular with some audiences but not with others. There is good content to be found out there through universities, independent subject-matter experts and specialist content providers, like LinkedIn Learning, that provide a broad range of topics.

Just be careful what you choose – always keep your ONE THING in mind. You can also use these avenues to note any future ONE THINGs you come across in you research.

UPSIDES	DOWNSIDES	THINGS TO CONSIDER
WEBINARS		
Many are free

They cover a wide range of different topics

If you don't like it, you can turn it off

You get to ask and respond to questions | Sometimes 'free' means the person or company running the session may be trying to sell you something (which is fine, just know that)

Quality of presentation and information can be variable and may lack opportunity for interaction | Check the time zones –some great content may happen in the middle of the night, but sometimes signing up will get you access to watch it later |
| **MOOCS (MASSIVE OPEN ONLINE COURSES)** | | |
| Many are free or have free versions

Great range of topics

Can be sourced from some of the top universities in the world

Some have set course times while others are 'anytime' programs | Not all offer accreditation, if that's what you are looking for | Can offer peer-to-peer experiences as well |
| **ELEARNING** | | |
| Great design can support engagement with the topic

Enables checks of understanding

Anytime, anywhere | Unfortunately, you may associate it with compliance training you've done at every organisation you've ever joined

Design quality can vary | It's hugely variable and once you have had a poor experience it can scar you for life |

So now we know where to find the content that will inform you on what you will do now you have decided your ONE THING, how do you know if it will be good, or useful. Luckily, the next chapter can help identify what good looks like.

CHAPTER 9
WHAT DOES 'GOOD' CONTENT LOOK LIKE?

It had long since come to my attention that people of accomplishment rarely sat back and let things happen to them. They went out and happened to things.

LEONARDO DA VINCI

It's never been easier to find information. You can simply take your Smartphone out of your pocket and find out something about anything you want to know. It's true that 'information is out there … you just have to let it in' (even though that may be an expression I heard from a less-than-mediocre TV cop show). But how do we know if we have 'let the right one in' (and okay, that's a movie title) and found information that is useful? While we have become reliant on the convenience of our many internet-connected devices, what we can't rely on is the quality of the information and whether it is the most useful approach to take as we travel on our ONE THING journey.

Let's look at what to do when considering information. It's a great idea to ask questions and interrogate the information a little by looking at the author, their intention, how the material is presented and particularly by checking the accuracy. Equally, examining our own thinking processes to minimise our cognitive and perceptual bias is important. It's about looking at what's out there in the world – and also what's already in our heads.

Critical thinking

Whether we are watching screen-based media like videos or eLearns; reading text in physical or online books, newspapers, and magazines; listening to others in conversation, on a podcast, or through an audiobook; or directly observing people and situations, we need to be able to think critically about the material. Let me be clear: critical thinking is not about having an argument or criticising others, it's about the tools we use to reflect on and get clarity about what we believe.

What do we mean by critical thinking and how do we know if we are doing it? The California Critical Thinking Disposition Inventory (CCTDI)[68] is a psychological test that is used to measure whether or not people are disposed to think critically. It focuses on the seven different thinking dispositions listed below, and it can be useful to ask ourselves to what extent they describe the way we think.

1. **Truthseeking:** *a disposition towards truth or bias*
   How determined are you to get a thorough understanding of a situation and doggedly track down the truth ... wherever it leads? Are you the 'no stone unturned' type, seeking solid evidence and applying logical reasoning? Or are you prone to bias and not keen to question your beliefs?

2. **Open-mindedness:** *a disposition toward open-mindedness or intolerance*
   Are you open to new ideas? Can you allow others to express their opinions, even if they don't align to your own – or especially when they don't? Or are you intolerant of others whose views do not align with your beliefs?

3. **Analyticity:** *a disposition toward anticipating possible consequences or being indifferent to them*
   Are you able to anticipate what's next? Do you analyse a situation and identify positive and negative consequences? Or do you act impulsively, unconcerned by consequences?

4. **Systematicity:** *a disposition toward proceeding in a systematic or unsystematic way*
   Do you approach things in a systematic way? Are you prone to break down complex problems into different aspects and work through your approach? Or is your thinking haphazard and undisciplined?

5. **Confidence in Reasoning:** *a disposition toward being confident or mistrustful of reasoned thinking*
   Are you confident in your reasoning? Do you see critical thinking, the use of reason and reflection as the best way to make decisions? Or do you defer to others and mistrust your ability to think things through rationally?

6. **Inquisitiveness:** *a disposition toward being inquisitive or resistant to learning*
   Are you naturally curious? If you don't know something, you need to find out – how it works, what it means, what comes next or just because? Or is it all a bit 'who cares'?

7. **Maturity of Judgment:** *a disposition toward considered judgment or simplistic thinking.*
   Are you able to balance thinking things through all the time knowing that you need to make a decision? Can you look at multiple perspectives and come to a conclusion? Or do you jump to conclusions, tend to think in black and white, or find you are incapable of deciding? Do you flip-flop with no good reason?

It's good to reflect on these questions and consider if there are things you do well, and things you could practice. Remember that as you progress through *Project You*, you will be finding information, discussing things with others, reflecting and experimenting. There is quite a lot of space for you to test out your reasoning for yourself and with the help of others.

One simple and practical thing a friend of mine uses is to take a pad (but you could use a laptop) and, as you are reviewing material, write down notes in three separate columns – one for what you find interesting, one for what you agree with, and one for what you don't agree with or are unsure about. Then interrogate these a little with some good conceptual questions. Why is it interesting? Why do I/don't I agree with this and how might I be wrong? This not only gives you a good basis for deciding the value of the material for yourself, it also locks the information in your head more effectively.

To help you do this, in the next section we will look at how our brains work for and against us when we are thinking: welcome to the mind-blowing world of cognitive bias.

Unconscious bias

Our brains are really very helpful. Whenever they can, they like to conserve energy by making some rules and assumptions about things we deal with regularly. Mostly, that's pretty smart and a good thing. If you had to take in every single piece of information you perceive as if it were the first time you encountered it and then try to figure out what was going on, your head would explode. However, sometimes these assumptions lead us up the garden path only to find a very wrong conclusion. This unfortunate, but kindly intended, adaptation is called 'unconscious bias'.

There are 150 or so identified biases, at the moment, but the number increases regularly. In chapter 6 we introduced you to the Dunning-Kruger effect, a bias that shows how we can be quite poor at estimating our abilities. Understanding unconscious biases, how they affect you and how to overcome the detrimental effects of this unhelpful help the brain provides us isn't an easy thing to do. That's because they are unconscious. Here we are, diligently looking for some good reliable information to help us develop ourselves while our own brains can simply be working against us.

Let's look more closely at one particular bias that effects how we think about what makes a good source of information for our ONE THING. Sometimes we get an idea into our heads about something that we think is important or will work well and then we go out and get evidence to prove we are right. This is called 'confirmation bias', and it happens a lot – it's natural, if lazy, thinking.

For example, something you observe that Mindy does at the office makes you suspect that she is bringing a cat to work. Because you suspect this, your brain automatically starts to look for positive signs you are right – Mindy's trip to the supermarket for cat food, extended periods of time away from her desk, the fur on her jacket that wasn't there this morning. It also ignores other possibilities, like Mindy might be minding her friend's apartment – complete with pets – located a few blocks away from the office. Okay, a random example, but you see how easily this could get out of hand.

Just as you don't take everything you read, watch or hear for granted, don't take everything you think for granted. The brain can be lazy – because it's trying to be helpful and save you energy – and takes shortcuts that sometimes lead to poor outcomes. On your journey into finding great ideas to apply to your professional development, make sure you aren't overlooking other perspectives by consciously slowing your thinking down and testing your underlying assumptions. You can think of it as looking for counterfactuals, which just means asking yourself: 'If my idea was wrong, what would I expect to find to prove that?' You should check out some more of these biases, many of which come with some great names. Dan Ariely's book, *Predictably Irrational*, is a lovely place to start.[69]

Assessing your information

So how do you assess information in such a content-rich environment? We need to find out whether it's gold or CRAAP ... and I mean that as an acronym. 'CRAAP' is a pneumonic device used to think about information. It stands for currency, relevance, authority, accuracy and purpose. It's most often used by students researching and writing papers. Here, we're adapting it for our purposes – because who doesn't like a great acronym – to help us broaden our thinking about the reliability, competence and integrity of the resources we use.

Currency

Check when your information was published or posted. Keep in mind this may matter when looking for guidance about developing your ONE THING or it may not. Some great information on specific subjects is by great thinkers and considered classic, and has valuable lessons for learners despite being written a while ago.

For example, you wouldn't necessarily expect to read about latest trends in neuroscience from something published in the 1980s, but you might read Robert B. Cialdini's book on influence, *Influence: the new psychology of modern persuasion*,[70] from that era and still find it relevant (although the words 'new' and 'modern' have been taken out of the title in recent editions). Mostly, you are looking for something between good, best and cutting-edge practice.

Relevance

Consider whether or not your information is about your topic and delivered in a way that you can understand. A scientific report may be exactly what you need to write a dissertation, but if you are not an academic researcher, it might be better to look for things that are intended for a more general audience – at least at first. You may decide to get deeper into the topic at some stage and consider resources targeted more to industry or researchers. Once again, don't be limited to thinking in terms of the written text – there'll be relevant information in a myriad of formats out there that can shape your learning. Just remember to stay on topic and choose a style that suits you.

Authority

Always make sure that the people responsible for the resource you are looking at know something about the content. Start with verifiable sources, those who are recognised as knowing about your ONE THING. If you are not so sure, or it's hard to ascertain, factor that in when you are weighing up what they are saying. There may still be a useful idea there that you can build on (remember, it doesn't always matter where you get that idea as long as it inspires you), but perhaps check your thinking with others and look for different opinions.

Accuracy

We don't have time for a treatise on the nature of truth just now, sorry, but you'll definitely want to know the information you are looking at is accurate. It helps to check the information you have found in a couple of sources to see if there is a degree of consistency. Can you easily identify what sort of evidence the information is based on? Also, is the content a little vague in relation to the subject? If so, try to find it somewhere else that could offer it in a bit more detail.

Purpose

Information is produced by people just like you and me. They have reasons for putting their stuff out there. But it's a good idea to consider the intention behind any information you discover. Perhaps it's just entertainment, or a satirical site or publication – which would make it a little unreliable for current best practice in your ONE THING. Possibly it has been specifically designed to educate and it's provided in a digestible form without bias and a range of perspectives. Sweet. Or maybe the people behind that interesting bit of content you've found have a product to sell – that's okay, just remember to factor that into your thinking.

Where to now?

A gentle reminder: in this chapter, we have been talking about how to find specific information for your ONE THING from subject-matter experts with impeccable experience and credentials. We've discovered that getting deep into your ONE THING is great as you work towards mastering it, but it's also good to stay curious about a range of things you're interested in as this can reveal quite unexpected options. We never know when something from an unrelated source could be the breakthrough that changes our world.

Thomas Kuhn, the American philosopher of science who identified the concept of the 'paradigm shift' over 50 years ago, is quoted as saying: ' individuals who break through by inventing a new paradigm are almost always either very young ... or very new to the field whose paradigm they change'.[71]

Best selling author Liz Wiseman calls this 'rookie smarts'. She is quoted as saying:

> When the world is changing quickly, experience can become a curse, trapping us in old ways of doing and knowing, while inexperience can be a blessing, freeing us to improvise and adapt quickly to changing circumstances.[72]

Now, it may sound a bit paradoxical (especially after just banging on about the need for reliable information) but remember that you can learn from many different sources – a trusted advisor, a dog peeing on a lamppost, a researcher with a PhD, a successful business person, your gran. Be aware that opportunities for learning are everywhere – you just have to be ready to take advantage of them. What matters is whether or not what you learn helps you change what you do, or influences who you are, in a positive way. Because that's the aim of *Project You* – to affect positive change in your life.

So we've looked at the how, why and what of learning, established how to choose and find information for your ONE THING, and you're ready to give something a red-hot go. It's now time for you to do the actual work on your ONE THING.

CONCLUSION
PUTTING IT ALL TOGETHER

Here it is ... the *iDevelop* guide to *Project You*. This section summarises everything we've been looking at and how it fits together. Whichever way you have chosen to work through this book – from the first page to this one; to picking out the things that interest you or that you need right now; or to jumping straight to the end, let's get clear on how it can work for you.

Here we have a step-by-step guide to using the information in this book. It's designed to set you up to learn ONE THING after another, develop a reflective practice and an experimental mindset, engage others to help you, and, once you have done your learning, to encourage you to help and inspire others with their own development.

If you feel you have read enough and just want to get started, there's a short version of our guide at the end of this section. For those who like a slightly more detailed overview, here it is!

Decide and identify

Decide
to start

Get clear
on your 'why'

What is your
ONE THING

The first phase is concerned with committing to the process. Every journey begins with a single step and your first one is deciding you want to take a journey. The word 'decide' comes from the Latin for 'to cut off'. You literally need to cut off other options – but just for now. Commit to giving your ONE THING – and *Project You* – a red-hot go, even if it takes you where you don't expect.

Identify your compelling 'Why'. Understanding why you want to do this will help enormously. How do you want to change? How do you want to do things differently and better? A compelling reason for any change you are planning will help you stay motivated through any moments of doubt or difficulty. If that's sounding 'pretty heavy, dude', keep in mind that, although this is important, it doesn't have to be serious. We do better when we play lightly with our learning. But you do need to know why you are doing this. Your ONE THING doesn't have to be big, or the most important, or the only thing – it's just ONE of a range of THINGS you will be working on over the course of *Project You*. Remember, we are trying to change your world, not the whole world (yet) and that we need to get very clear on what that change is driven by.

Observe and plan

Start your reflective practice | Find information | What might get in the way | Map out your plan | Create your milestones

Having decided on your ONE THING, you'll need to turn to *Project You*. This is where you start your reflective practice. Keep an eye out for where, how and when you are currently doing your ONE THING. In this phase, you are not changing anything – you are learning to understand. Ask yourself questions, query your judgement and remember: your reflective practice can include others, so start to build *The Team*.

Now, you don't have to do this all at once. Try doing it gradually. Look for the appropriate people who can guide or assist you as you begin to notice where you might need a new perspective. Choose people who are likely to prevent you from falling foul of any unconscious biases that crop up in your thinking, or any mental schema that could impact on your progress.

Begin gathering information. If you get some helpful advice, put it to one side for now until you get a very clear picture of what you need to do. Start reading, listening, watching and collecting good content about best, or at least useful, practice for your ONE THING. Continue to build your knowledge and understanding.

When you discover something new that looks valuable, ask yourself: if this is such a good idea, why aren't I doing it already?

What might be getting in my way? What are the payoffs for keeping things the same? It's better to identify things that might get in the way of your success now before you get too far in the process.

At this point, say 'well done' to yourself for not jumping right in, for taking a little bit of time to get clear on what you want to do. You're now ready to map things out further. What are you going to change, and how are you going to change it? When is this likely to happen? Who can help by giving you feedback? With these questions in mind, make your plan. What do you need to do first? What do you need to after that? Plan it out using whatever method floats your boat: a detailed Excel spreadsheet, a drawing, a Kanban, a list – as long as it works for you.

Remember, your plan is a sequence of things you will do. It's a sequence of actions that happen in a certain order that you set out. Choose some milestones to put in along the way, things that confirm you are on the right path. They won't be the final goal, but they should be meaningful achievements for you to aim for along the way.

You could create a list of milestones by asking yourself: 'If I apply...', sorry... '*When* I apply what I have learnt to make a positive difference, how will I know? What will it look like? What is success in this instance?' Your milestones should be meaningful to you. They don't all need to be done, or done in order. They're there for you to know when you should push a little further, or when you should give yourself a little pat on the back for achieving them.

I like the idea that academics Dan and Chip Heath discuss in their book, *The Power of Moments*,[73] where they create levels of achievement, like in an online game. As you 'level-up' you increase the degree of difficulty. In an example inspired by their work for learning a foreign language, Level 1 might be signing up for a class; Level 2 might be when you are courageous enough to greet a native speaker you know from your neighbourhood in their language; Level 3 might be the first time you can understand a headline of a newspaper in that language you notice at the newsagency; and Level 4 would be when you read your first book in that language.

Identifying these levels before carrying out your learning can serve to spur you into action. So, make some meaningful, funny, exciting, exotic milestones. They all lead you to your destination – in this example, being able to hold a conversation in a foreign language with a native speaker – and give you ways inspire you and celebrate along the way.

Act and embed

Now start your active practice

Continue reflective practice

Seek some feedback

Get it to stick

The next stage involves you applying what you know. Congratulations! People often find themselves falling into the deep dark abyss that is the knowing-doing gap, so even getting here is pretty darn brilliant. It's crucial at this point to maintain your reflective practice and to get feedback from *The Team*.

If things don't go as well as you like, or as quickly as you like (and what are the odds on that) *The Team* should be there to help you. You may need Aunt Edna in your head to give you some encouragement. Sometimes you'll need *The Team* to hold you to account, and then a small dose of Aunt Doris may not go astray either – just to keep you in check. Keep trying and keep perspective. It is going to take a while to get your learning to stick. Use every trick in the book (this book especially) to make this new way a habit, the new business-as-usual, to permanently, and then continuously, improve your state. At times, this process will go great. At others, it's going to fall over. It may even whistle Dixie. Just don't stop being curious and being surprised about how it will challenge and change you.

Thanks, next

Celebrate with your team

Whats next?

It's very important to be grateful to those who support you – and to show it. That includes you and *The Team*. Think about what went well, what didn't; the good advice and the well-intentioned, but not-so-good, advice. Be in awe a little about the amazing ability we have as human beings to make change. Revel in the support we can be for each other.

Be a little inventive with how you say 'thanks' to *The Team*. You don't need to give them merry bushels of cash, expensive gifts or a big party. But be thoughtful and as generous as you can. One of the best ways to do that is to keep being you, keep learning more and following their example by supporting others as they learn. You too could be part of someone else's *Team*. So, say 'Thanks', say 'What's next?' and look around for who needs *your* help. This isn't about you charging in on your white horse to save everyone – especially any learning deniers you see nearby – from themselves, it's much subtler than that, but don't worry – you'll figure it out.

Oh, my word! Stop me as I am about to say this is a 'never-ending journey' … but the thing is, it actually is. I want to wish you good luck on that journey, even if you try just ONE THING from this book rather than the whole shebangi. Good luck! Continue to learn and use what you know to do great things.

Project You at a glance

THE PROJECT YOU GUIDE		
DECIDE AND IDENTIFY		
	Decide to start	Every journey begins with a single step. The first step is deciding you want to take a journey. Commit to giving it a red-hot-go, even if it takes you where you don't expect.
	Get clear on your 'why'	Define your compelling reason for the change you are planning. It will keep you motivated and help you through any moments of doubt.
	Choose your ONE THING	Remember, we are trying to change your world, not the whole world; be clear and specific about the ONE THING you want to learn
OBSERVE AND PLAN		
	Start your reflective practice	Start observing yourself and how you go about your ONE THING.
	Find information	Other people and some reliable data sources can help clarify your ONE THING. Plus, ask the peeps you respect and value if they will be on *The Team* and share their observations on your progress along the way.
	Identify what might get in the way	Prepare for the things you foresee that might stop you, including any hidden beliefs unearthed in you along the way.
	Map out your plan	Knowing what you know now, plan what you are going to do, what you will try and how to apply your new focus.
	Create your milestones	Make a list of what you expect to see happen if this ONE THING goes well. You don't need to do them all, you don't need to do them in order, just keep doing the work and keep an eye out for achievement.

	ACT AND EMBED	
🏃	Now start your active practice	Here we go - the experiment starts here. It's time to implement what you know.
👤	Continue reflective practice	Check in with yourself regularly on how things are working out.
💬	Seek some feedback	Keep in touch with *The Team* and get their perspectives on how things are going.
🔒	Get it to stick	Make what you are learning a habit, your usual response, or the 'new you'. Lock your ONE THING in with practise, repetition and using any hacks that work for you.
	THANKS, NEXT	
🎈	Celebrate with your team!	Whether you succeeded in learning something new, or reworking something old, take a moment to feel a bit good about it. Make sure you let those brave enough to hold you to account and give you support know what that means to you.
👉	What's next?	Don't stop now!

ENDNOTES

1. hbr.org/2015/12/4-ways-to-become-a-better-learner
2. joshbersin.com/2010/06/how-to-build-a-high-impact-learning-culture/
3. www.gallup.com/workplace/244628/why-time-disrupt-traditional-approach.aspx
4. www.gallup.com/workplace/244628/why-time-disrupt-traditional-approach.aspx
5. www.theschooloflife.com/thebookoflife/we-only-learn-if-we-repeat/
6. www.gallup.com/workplace/244628/why-time-disrupt-traditional-approach.aspx
7. Dr Lila Davachi, Dr Tobias Kiefer, Dr David Rock and Lisa Rock, 'Learning that lasts through AGES', *NeuroLeadership Journal*, Issue 3, 2010.
8. Ibid., 5
9. Ibid., 5
10. Ibid., 7
11. David A Kolb, *Experiential learning: experience as the source of learning and development*, FT Press, 1983.
12. Carol S Dweck, *Mindset: The new psychology of success*, Ballantine Books, New York, 2016.
13. John Whitmore, *Coaching for performance: GROWing human potential and purpose*, 4th ed., Nicholas Brealey Publishing, London, 2010.
14. Marshall Goldsmith, *What got you here won't get you there*, Profile Books, London, 2012.

15 John Dewey, *How we think*, D.C. Heath & Co., Publishers, 1910.

16 Giada Di Stefano, Francesca Gino, Gary P Pisano, Bradley R Staats, 'Making experience count: the role of reflection in individual learning', Harvard Business School Working Paper, 14-093, 2016, p. 26.

17 Ibid., p. 26.

18 Matthew D Lieberman, *Social: why our brains are wired to connect*, Crown Publishers, New York, 2013, p. 22.

19 Linda Lawrence-Wilkes and Lyn Ashmore, *The reflective practitioner in professional education*, Palgrave Macmillan, Basingstoke, United Kingdom, 2014.

20 Jennifer Porter, 'Why you should make time for self-reflection (even if you hate doing it)', *Harvard Business Review*, 21 March 2017.

21 David Rock, *Your brain at work*, HarperCollins, New York, 2009.

22 hbr.org/2018/05/learning-is-a-learned-behavior-heres-how-to-get-better-at-it

23 Caroline Webb, *How to have a good day: the essential toolkit for a productive day at work and beyond*, Pan Books, London, 2017, pp 87-88.

24 hbr.org/2018/01/what-self-awareness-really-is-and-how-to-cultivate-it

25 Gary Rolfe, Dawn Freshwater and Melanie Jasper, *Critical reflection in nursing and the helping professions: a user's guide*, Basingstoke, Palgrave Macmillan, 2001.

26 www.tinyhabits.com/

27 John Ruskin, *The Crown of Wild Olive*, Lecture IV: 'The Future of England', section 151, 1866.

28 hbr.org/2017/01/a-3-step-plan-for-turning-weaknesses-into-strengths

29 startupbros.com/overthinkers-guide-taking-action-complete-guide/

30 Susan Jeffers, *Feel the fear and do it anyway*, Harcourt, California, 1987

31 www.susanjeffers.com/home/5truths.cfm

32 www.physicsclassroom.com/class/newtlaws/Lesson-1/Newton-s-First-Law

33 www.facebook.com/TonyRobbins/posts/10154720220389060

34 startupbros.com/overthinkers-guide-taking-action-complete-guide/

35 startupbros.com/overthinkers-guide-taking-action-complete-guide/

36 www.positivityblog.com/how-to-take-more-action-9-powerful-tips/

37 Robert Kegan and Lisa Lahey Laskow, *Immunity to change*, Harvard Business Press, Boston, 2009.

38 Marianne Williamson, *A return to love: reflections on the principles of a course in miracles*, Harper Collins, 1992, pp 190-191.

39 L. S. Vygotsky,'The genesis of higher mental functions', in R. Reiber (ed.), *The history of the development of higher mental functions*, vol. 4, pp 97-120, Plennum, New York, 1987.

40 hbr.org/2016/03/learning-to-learn

41 www.verywellmind.com/an-overview-of-the-dunning-kruger-effect-4160740

42 hbr.org/2016/03/learning-to-learn

43 David Rock, *Your brain at work*, HarperCollins, New York, 2009.

44 Matthew D Lieberman, *Social: why our brains are wired to connect*, Crown Publishers, New York, 2013, p. 22.

45 Naomi I Eisenberger and Matthew D Lieberman, 'Why rejection hurts: a common neural alarm system for physical and social pain', *Trends in Cognitive Sciences*, vol.8, no.7, July 2004.

46 experiencelife.com/article/the-power-of-curiosity/

47 Patrick Lencioni, *The advantage: why organisational health trumps everything else in business*, Jossey-Bass, San Francisco, 2012.

48 Heidi Grant-Halvorson, *No one understands you and what to do about it*, Harvard Business Review Press, Boston, 2015.

49 David Rock, 'SCARF: a brain-based model for collaborating with and influencing others', *NeuroLeadership Journal*, Issue 1, 2008.

50 Tessa West, 'Next in performance: feedback management', NeuroLeadership Institute Summit 2017, October 2017, New York.

51 E Gilbert, *Big Magic: Creative Living Beyond Fear, Riverhead Books*, New York, 2015.

52 James Clear, *Atomic Habits: an easy and proven way to build good habits and break bad ones*, Avery, New York, p. 41, 2018.

53 Daniel H Pink, *Drive: the surprising truth about what motivates us*, Riverhead Books, New York, 2011.

54 James Clear, *Atomic Habits: an easy and proven way to build good habits and break bad ones*, Avery New York, 2018, p. 30.

55 Ibid., p. 33.

56 hbr.org/2014/05/from-purpose-to-impact

57 Mihaly Csikszentmihalyi, *Finding flow: the psychology of engagement with everyday life*, Basic Books, New York, 1997.

58 James Clear, *Atomic Habits*, 2018, p. 227

59 Marcus Buckingham and Donald O Clifton, *Now, discover your strengths*, Pocket Books, 2005, p. 6.

60 Tomas Chamorro-Premuzic, 'Stop focusing on your strengths', *Harvard Business Review*, 21 January 2016.

61 zengerfolkman.com/white-papers/developing-strengths-or-weaknesses/

62 Lynne Cazaly, *ish: The problem with our pursuit for perfection and the life-changing practice of good enough*, self-published, Australia, 2019

63 hbr.org/2018/11/if-you-want-to-get-better-at-something-ask-yourself-these-two-questions

64 hbr.org/2018/07/take-control-of-your-learning-at-work

65 http://theprintingreport.com/2018/05/03/the-rise-in-popularity-of-printed-books-continues/

66 This is a small part of the trend to open-source research that aims to share the findings of scientific endeavours more widely and freely in the hope that others will build on existing work.

67 Blinkist is currently a popular example.

68 https://philosophy.hku.hk/think/critical/improve.php, https://www.rand.org/education-and-labor/projects/assessments/tool/1992/california-critical-thinking-disposition-inventory.html

69 Dan Ariely, Predictably Irrational, HarperCollins, 2008.

70 Robert B Cialdini, *Influence: the new psychology of modern persuasion*, Quill, New York, 1984.

71 Thomas S Kuhn, *The structure of scientific revolutions*, University of Chicago Press, Chicago, 1962

72 Liz Wiseman, *Rookie smarts: why learning beats knowing in the new game of work*, Harper Business, 2014

73 Chip Heath and Dan Heath, *The power of moments: why certain experiences have extraordinary impact*, Simon & Schuster, New York, Chapter 8, 2017

INDEX

B
behavioural change, 50, 98
belief mapping, 74
Big Five of Learning, 14-17
Boser, Ulrich, 54
Bregman, Peter, 117

C
California Critical Thinking Disposition Inventory, the, 138
Chan, Amy, 38
Clear, James, 59, 96, 97, 114
cognitive bias, 79, 138, 141
cognitive quiet, 54
confirmation bias, 142
conscious competence model, 29-32, 41
continual professional development, 20-21
CRAAP
    currency, relevance, authority, accuracy and purpose, 143
Craig, Nick, 99-100
critical thinking, 91, 138-140

D
Dewey, John, 51, 160
Drucker, Peter, 43
Dunning-Kruger effect, 79, 141, 161
Dweck, Carol, 27, 40-41, 159

E
Eschenroeder, Kyle, 65, 67

F
failure, 69, 70, 72-74
feedback
    360°, 63, 111, 122
    giving, 88-90
    receiving, 8, 11, 15, 28, 46, 64, 85-89, 90-92
    seeking 85, 88, 90-92
Fogg, B.J., 59

G
Grant-Halvorson, Heidi, 90, 161

H
Heath, Dan and Chip, 152-153, 160, 162
Hoffer, Eric, 38

J
Jeffers, Susan, 65-66, 160

K
Kegan, Robert, 69, 161
knowing-doing gap, 61, 153
Kolb, David, 34-35, 45, 159
Kuhn, Thomas, 146, 162

L
Lawrence-Wilkes, Linda, 52, 160
Lahey, Lisa, 69, 161
learning
    conscious, 2, 6-7
    deniers, 1, 2, 5, 155
    formal, 1, 19-20, 37, 41, 119
    independent, 5, 63, 121
    models
        70:20:10, 27, 36-38, 119
        iDevelop Learning, 4, 6, 11, 45-46, 63, 122
        Rolfe's Reflective Model, 58, 160
        Transfer of Learning, 39
    self-directed, 4, 41
    social learning, 5, 11, 37, 46, 48, 63, 122
Learning Agency, the, 54
Lencioni, Patrick, 89, 161
Lewins, Kurt, 7

Lieberman, Matthew D., 52, 160, 161

M
meta-cognition, 53, 80
mindfulness, 53, 54
mindsets
    fixed, 26-29
    growth, 26-29, 40

N
NeuroLeadership Institute, the, 33, 54
neuroscience, 8, 26, 32, 143

O
ONE THING, 7-11, 15, 29, 41, 48, 49, 52-53, 56-59, 62, 64, 67, 68, 74-78, 95-97, 101-102, 107, 109, 114-118, 150-151, 156

P
Peterson, David, 10
Pink, Dan, 96, 161
Porter, Jennifer, 53, 160
professional development, 3, 6, 13, 23, 38, 109, 142
Project You, 6-11, 14, 17, 21, 48, 55, 64, 74, 76, 95-97, 151

R
reflective practice, 4, 47, 51-60, 63, 122
Robbins, Tony, 67, 160
Rock, Dr David, 54, 159, 161

S
Snook, Scott, 99-100

T
Team, the, 8-9, 11, 17, 49, 57, 64, 77, 81-86, 92-93, 107, 151, 153, 154-156

W
Webb, Caroline, 55, 160
Wiseman, Liz, 146, 162

Z
Ziglar, Zig, 23

www.ingramcontent.com/pod-product-compliance
Lightning Source LLC
Chambersburg PA
CBHW031419290426
44110CB00011B/453